The Civic Life of American Religion

The Civic Life of
American Religion

Edited by Paul Lichterman and C. Brady Potts

Stanford University Press
Stanford, California

Stanford University Press
Stanford, California

Printed in the United States of America on acid-free, archival-quality paper

Library of Congress Cataloging-in-Publication Data

Lichterman, Paul.
   The civic life of American religion / edited by Paul Lichterman and C. Brady Potts.
     p.   cm.
   Includes bibliographical references and index.
   ISBN 978-0-8047-5795-9 (cloth : alk. paper)—ISBN
978-0-8047-5796-6 (pbk. : alk. paper)
    1. Religion and civil society—United States.   2. Religion and sociology—United States.
  3. Voluntarism—Religious aspects.   I. Potts, C. Brady (Charles Brady)   II. Title.
   BL60.L54 2008
    306.60973—dc22   2008016631

Typeset by Westchester Book Group in 10/14 Minion

Contents

Acknowledgments   vii

Contributors   ix

1 The Civic Life of American Religion:
   An Introductory Statement   1
   Paul Lichterman and C. Brady Potts

2 The Varieties of Civic Experience   23
   Michael Schudson

3 Building Religious Communities, Building the
   Common Good: A Skeptical Appreciation   48
   Nancy Ammerman

4 Congregations' Significance to American Civic Life   69
   Mark Chaves

5 Beyond Savior, Victim, and Sinner: Neighborhood Civic
   Life and "Absent Presence" in the Religious District   82
   Omar M. McRoberts

6 How Religion Circulates in America's Local Public Square   100
   Paul Lichterman

7 A Tacit Sense of Evil? The Meaning of Politics in
   United Methodist Debates over Homosexuality   123
   Dawne Moon

8   Conclusion: Rethinking Religion's Civic Life   140
Paul Lichterman and C. Brady Potts

Index   157

Acknowledgments

THE CENTER FOR RELIGION AND CIVIC CULTURE at the University of Southern California has done much to make this book possible. We thank Don Miller, Executive Director of the center, and Jon Miller, Director of Research, for lending their infectious enthusiasm to the project. They and the rest of the center's executive board generously agreed to sponsor focused conversations that would help us think in creative and disciplined ways about how religion inhabits civic life. We're grateful to all our conversation partners and to Brie Loskota and Tim Sato for adroit administrative assistance. At Stanford University Press, Kate Wahl appreciated the importance of our topic and was a marvelous shepherd. Anonymous outside reviewers saw conceptual connections as well as glitches that we had missed and helped us craft sharper, fuller introductory and concluding chapters.

Contributors

NANCY AMMERMAN has spent much of the last decade studying American religious organizations. Her book *Pillars of Faith: American Congregations and Their Partners* (University of California Press, 2005) describes the common organizational patterns that shape the work of America's diverse communities of faith. She previously wrote extensively on conservative religious movements, including *Baptist Battles: Social Change and Religious Conflict in the Southern Baptist Convention*, which received the 1992 SSSR Distinguished Book Award. Nancy is professor of sociology of religion at Boston University, where she teaches in both the Sociology Department and the School of Theology. She was the 2004–5 president of the Society for the Scientific Study of Religion.

MARK CHAVES has a Master of Divinity degree from Harvard Divinity School and a PhD in Sociology from Harvard University. He is professor of sociology, religion, and divinity at Duke University. Among other projects, he directs the National Congregations Study (NCS), a wide-ranging survey of a nationally representative sample of religious congregations. His most recent book, based largely on the 1998 NCS, is *Congregations in America* (Harvard, 2004). Data collection for Wave II of the NCS was completed in spring 2007. He has been chair of the American Sociological Association's Sociology of Religion Section, and in 2008 he begins his term as president of the Society for the Scientific Study of Religion.

PAUL LICHTERMAN is currently associate professor of sociology and religion at the University of Southern California. He writes on culture, religion, civic and political organizations, social and cultural theory, and ethnographic methodology. His second book, *Elusive Togetherness: Church Groups*

Trying to Bridge America's Divisions (Princeton University Press, 2005), is a study of religious community service groups responding to welfare reform. The book depicts how these groups tried hard yet quite often failed to create enduring ties with other civic groups, state agencies, and low-income people. It received the 2006 Distinguished Book Award from the Society for the Scientific Study of Religion and the 2006 Distinguished Scholarship Award from the Pacific Sociological Association. Before coming to the University of Southern California in fall 2004, he was associate professor of sociology at the University of Wisconsin–Madison.

OMAR M. McROBERTS's scholarly and teaching interests include the sociology of religion, urban sociology, urban poverty, race, and collective action. His first book, *Streets of Glory: Church and Community in a Black Urban Neighborhood*, was published by the University of Chicago Press (2003). The book is based on an ethnographic study of religious life in Four Corners, a poor, predominantly black neighborhood in Boston containing twenty-nine congregations. It explains the high concentration, wide variety, and ambiguous social impact of religious activity in the neighborhood. McRoberts is currently conducting a study of black religious responses to, and influences on, social welfare policy since the New Deal, culminating with George W. Bush's Office of Faith Based and Community Initiatives. He is also initiating an ethnographic project on cultures of death and dying among black congregations in low-income urban contexts.

DAWNE MOON has taught courses on religion, gender, sexuality, and qualitative methods at the University of California, Berkeley, and Marquette University. Her main interest is in how people develop the ideas that mean the most to them and the impacts those ideas have on social life. She is the author of *God, Sex and Politics: Homosexuality and Everyday Theologies* (University of Chicago Press, 2004), which ethnographically examines how members of two United Methodist congregations develop their ideas about God, community, and sexual morality. She is currently studying American Jews' understandings and experiences of anti-Semitism, especially as those ideas relate to politics, identity, and community.

C. BRADY POTTS is a PhD student in Sociology at the University of Southern California. His areas of interest include the culture of U.S. public life and theories of civil society. He received his master's degree in sociology at the University of Wisconsin–Madison in 2004. His current research focuses on public speech and political culture in the aftermath of natural disasters.

MICHAEL SCHUDSON is distinguished professor of communication and adjunct professor of sociology at the University of California, San Diego, and professor of communication at the Graduate School of Journalism, Columbia University. He received his PhD in sociology from Harvard. He is the author of six books on the history and sociology of the American news media, advertising, popular culture, and politics and cultural memory. His honors include a Guggenheim Fellowship and a MacArthur Foundation Award. His most recent work is *The Sociology of News* (Norton, 2003) and *The Good Citizen: A History of American Civic Life* (1998). The latter offers an original interpretation of the historical transformation of both the practices and the ideals of civic participation. It has been reviewed not only in academic publications in sociology, history, and political science but in general publications like the *Washington Post* and *The Economist*.

1 The Civic Life of American Religion: An Introductory Statement

Paul Lichterman and C. Brady Potts

THE YEAR 1967 WAS A REMARKABLE one for students of religion. Three prominent sociologists, Peter Berger, Thomas Luckmann, and Talcott Parsons, each published sweeping statements on the fate of religion in modern societies, with the United States particularly in mind. Though their prognoses differed, each was announcing that religion as many people understood it was disappearing from public life. Their assessments became common sense for many sociologists and represented the common sense of many Americans and perhaps many citizens in the modern West.[1]

If one were to condense these scholars' statements into a simple credo, it might sound like this: Ordinary, modern people keep their religion to themselves. We hear religion in religious congregations, not in public life beyond sanctuary walls—apart from the occasional, vestigial reference to a nondenominational God at presidential inaugurations and other high rituals of the nation. When it comes to expressing ultimate priorities publicly, we talk mostly about abstract values, such as individual freedom, equal opportunity, and compassion, but not religion in the sense of old traditions that claim to access the divine. Those people who affirm traditional religion often do so more out of rote than conviction anyway. Religious groups and institutions have an old but largely quiet place in American public life, caring for the needy who show up on their doorsteps and promoting upstanding American citizenship.

The credo would be short because there would not be much else to say.

The truth value of this creed and the subtler sociological thinking it condenses was debatable forty years ago, and it misapprehends wide swaths of American public life since then. Religions—not general values but particular, passionate faiths—were moving many thousands of Americans to civil rights activism the year that the three statements on religion appeared. Over the next several decades, a formidable Christian conservative political movement grew. It not only influenced elections for local school board members, governors, and presidents but also refigured many Americans' everyday conversations and energized social activism on different sides of many social issues in local as well as national forums. And local congregations and religious coalitions continued participating in the less dramatic rounds of local public life, advocating for urban development, protesting pornography, sponsoring forums on nuclear weapons or civil wars in Central America.[2]

The collective common sense in sociology has been catching up with events, as an accumulating body of research has made the creed of privatized religion difficult to uphold. Many students of public religion now would point out that religion never really did go private or transmute entirely into secular abstractions. We are discovering that religion is a normal—not necessarily virtuous, or divisive, or overwhelmingly influential, or decorative and ineffectual, but normal—part of American civic life. In the chapters that follow, six scholars assess the limits and potentials of the civic life of religion. This is a crucial time to do that. First let's introduce the civic realm and the place of religious associations there.

What Is Civic Life?

Civic means any relationship in which people communicate with one another and work together relatively voluntarily as members of a community or a society. These are relationships that are not directly or primarily dictated by governmental or familial authority or by the routines of exchange in the market. In our definition, civic groups include such voluntary associations as the Kiwanis Clubs, Martin Luther King Jr. Day planning committees, and women's health collectives, and also Ku Klux Klan groups, nativist militias, the White Citizens' Council, and other groups whose practices depart sharply from many writers' ideal of civic life. Civic group members relate to one another as members of some larger, nonfamily collectivity, but they do not necessarily define themselves in inclusive terms. Different kinds of civic groups include or exclude to varying degrees.[3] For example, as Jason Kaufman argues in his historical study of American fraternal organizations and mutual aid societies, insofar as these groups have competed for members (often along ethnic lines) and focused on providing for members, we could say that fraternalism has taught Americans that "self-segregation [is] acceptable, if not preferable to cooperation and collectivization."[4] Not all civic groups are "fraternal" associations, but the larger point is that while civic groups pursue goals consonant with their vision of a good society, they do not always practice what many observers would call "civic virtue." *Civic*, then, will be a descriptive rather than a normative term for us.

Relationships or even brief conversations that we could call civic sometimes spring up among governmental or market actors: If county social workers participate in community service alliances directed by church leaders, they are participating in civic life even though they work for the state. This is why we distinguish civic associations from others by the kind of communication they host, the kind of relationships they sustain, rather than considering them a separate social "sector" or an arena of discrete groups, the way policymakers and nonprofit professionals sometimes do. When we say "civic groups," we have in mind groups, relationships or local institutions that could include, among others, community centers, service clubs, citizen advocacy groups, social movement organizations, nonprofit service providers, town hall forums, volunteer associations, e-mail discussion groups, churches, synagogues, mosques, and religiously based alliances.

As the long list suggests, American civic groups can take very different shapes. Some of these have become far more common while others have become less typical. Fifty years ago, many American civic groups were local chapters of national federations. People joined a local chapter, organized by other unpaid members, and they served a locale in general, or sometimes a religious or ethnic group in the locale. They joined such groups as the Elks clubs, League of Women Voters groups, or B'nai B'rith chapters that still exist today. Increasingly, civic groups are professionally run organizations that pursue particular issues or a particular social agenda with like-minded others rather than define themselves as serving the interests of a community as a whole. Often they join with other groups in short-term coalitions that emerge to fight a particular campaign or advocate the passage of a particular piece of legislation. Good examples are the Grey Panthers, Mothers Against Drunk Driving, or Greenpeace.[5]

Sociologists group together this wide variety of groups, associations, and networks and say that these constitute "civil society." In the simplest terms, civil society is the voluntary realm of social life outside the family, the economy, and the state.[6] We will use the term sparingly, though, because its connotation of an easily defined sector of society defies reality. As a shorthand term, "civic groups" refers to any relationships in which people treat each other and communicate to the wider society as citizens or members of a community or a society, rather than as clients or administrators of the state or consumers, producers, managers, or owners in the marketplace. They relate to each other "civically."

A Civic Lens on Religious Associations

Religious associations turn out to be old participants in civic life in the United States. In everyday conversation Americans often distinguish "civic" from "religious" the way we distinguish "secular" from "sacred," but religious groups are civic groups in widely accepted social-science terms. Prominent writers on civic life refer to congregations and other religious associations as important instances of civic life, as Michael Schudson points out in the next chapter. Religious associations—religiously sponsored volunteer groups, coalitions of congregations, or religious special issue or community service groups such as an interfaith homeless shelter network, in addition to congregations—count as civic in the United States because the government does not mandate participation in them, and participants communicate with one another as members of some (religiously defined) community or collectivity. While these groups may well cultivate religious piety or spiritual awakening in their members' private lives, this book is interested in them as associations, whose members more or less voluntarily fashion relations to one another and the wider world.

Religious congregations and associations may be the most widespread, and egalitarian, sites of civic engagement in the United States.[7] Almost half of Americans' association memberships are church related. Half of Americans' volunteering takes place in a religious context.[8] Religious groups long have participated in movements for social justice and local charitable service efforts. In different ways, religious commitments lead some Americans to civic engagement beyond their own congregations.[9] This book will not survey American religion's civic life exhaustively. Religious news broadcasts, music recordings, or e-lists are means to building relationships within and between faith communities. Religious media are important sites of religion's civic life that this short volume does not consider.

In secular academic contexts, it is easy to ask "why study religious groups if we are interested in civic life?" From the numbers alone one may as well ask why not study religious associations if we are interested in civic life. Of course, studies of local public religious groups are hardly new. Recently, though, more and more social scientists are studying religious associations, and not only congregations, as associations—as instances of local civic relationships, using the lens we are introducing here.[10]

Why Focus on Civic, Not Political, Associations?

Why study religion's local civic relationships instead of asking about religion's sometimes contentious presence in national electoral politics? Social philosopher Alexis de Tocqueville famously argued that American democracy depended at least as much on good associations as good government or good laws, and he distinguished political from civic associations.[11] Political associations, or "political society" as he called them, makeup the arena in which we often hear the nationally known, conservative Christian spokespersons and politicians that many Americans now imagine when someone says "religion in public." Political society is the realm of interest groups and political party organizations that exist expressly in order to win power in legislatures or fight for laws and policies favorable to their members. Few need to be convinced that religion influences some political associations in the contemporary United States.

Yet a scholarly radar attuned only to conservative Christian political figures and interest groups or national debates over abortion or gay marriage will miss a substantial part of religion's presence in U.S. public life. As Nancy Ammerman has found, religious congregation–based volunteers carry out a wide array of projects.[12] They house homeless adults and runaway teens, shelter battered women and children, serve hot meals to hungry people, donate clothing, assist victims of natural disasters, or join networks that advocate for affordable housing, neighborhood development, or gay and lesbian rights. Not only do religious civic associations do many things in public, but we can call some of what they do "political" if members are organizing a march, writing their congresspersons, discussing political issues, or trying to politicize issues such as homelessness by defining them in political terms—a right to housing, for example. We can say, too, that they are being political if they are trying to depoliticize issues, as when the church members discussed in Dawne Moon's chapter of this volume suppose that unquestionable ideas about what church is for, rather than open debate, should determine whether or not their congregation fully includes lesbians and gay men. Put simply, civic associations are political sometimes.

Sometimes the charitable efforts of local congregations and religious associations become very relevant to national politics, as when policymakers throughout the 1990s and into the new century argued that religious groups should do more social service work in place of governmental agencies. The "Charitable Choice" provision of welfare policy reform in 1996 and the subsequent "faith-based initiatives" program of the George W. Bush presidential administration starting in 2001 made strong implicit assumptions about what local religious groups could do for social service in the country at large, as Mark Chaves points out in this volume. These national policies increased opportunities for local groups to fund their service work with tax money.

Local religious associations matter, though, even when they are not the immediate object of political debate or tax support, and even if they are not discussing issues one can politicize easily. The "civic" lens helps us see this broader significance: Civic associations, religious as well as secular, are in theory places in which people may learn to care about and talk about public issues to begin with, including but certainly not limited to the "moral values" issues such as gay marriage or school prayer that are so hotly debated today. In theory, civic associations also are places in which people can learn to care about one another, and about other people and groups near and far.[13] In Tocqueville's spirit, some social scientists have looked to them as generators of new ideas and new feelings that keep citizens talking and working with each other. Whether or not civic associations always work this way, investigating these associations can tell us a lot about how people can talk about social and political issues, how people can organize the work of advocacy or care, when they are not immediately being constrained by interest group loyalties, political party mandates, or governmental regulations. Studying civic associations tells us about how broad or narrow people's social horizons can be.

Many people wonder about the future of American community life, and the future of American democracy. In Tocqueville's spirit they often have focused some of their hopes on the potentials of civic associations. Sociologist Theda Skocpol, for instance, has cautioned that democracy is diminished if ordinary citizens allow professionally run, narrowly defined interest groups to determine their public agendas for them. She has proposed that religiously based civic groups have a role in a new and better social contract that would unite diverse Americans and guarantee to serve everyone's basic needs. But what kinds of civic ties are Americans willing to create? Sociologist Robert Wuthnow finds that many Americans prefer "loose" civic connections over enduring ties. On the positive side, short-term, plug-in style volunteer work helps to keep community life alive in a highly mobile society. For Wuthnow it is an open question whether or not this in-and-out style of civic engagement can bridge social diversity and empower citizens to steer society. On the more pessimistic side, sociologist Robert Bellah and his research team found in the 1980s that many Americans preferred to sequester themselves in enclaves of the like-minded instead of taking responsibility for more encompassing communities. Communitarian theorist Amitai Etzioni has warned that Americans have indulged in narrow-minded identity politics instead of working together for the common good, and now desperately need to "remoralize" civil society by committing to core values. As public policy scholar Francis Fukuyama has viewed it, Americans' "radius of trust" has been shrinking over the last several decades, though he sees signs that Americans also could regenerate fraying social ties.[14]

Political scientist Robert Putnam's now-famous findings on civic engagement put this ongoing discussion of togetherness in America on a new footing. Writing in 2000, Putnam found that Americans joined far fewer civic groups, socialized less, and trusted public officials less than just three decades earlier. Figures on declining civic group memberships should trouble us, Putnam argued, because these groups generate the social networks, norms of reciprocity, and trust that make up "social capital." And social capital enables citizens to work together more easily on community projects, build cross-group alliances, or join together to hold government accountable.[15] Not only scholars fear for the health of civic America. Claims about the decline of civic groups resonate in everyday conversation, as many Americans have told researchers and pollsters that they worry that community is not as strong as it used to be.[16]

None of these commentators have said that local civic groups, whether secular or religious, could strengthen the social fabric by themselves. They have hoped, though, that religious associations could play a part in regenerating social ties that will empower citizens. None have advocated that the United States become a "Christian nation." They do think that given American culture and history, there are widely shared religious resources for civic engagement, and they consider religious groups important players in American civic life.

Optimists, Pessimists, and an Emerging Inquiry

Religion figured large in Tocqueville's arguments about the virtues of civic life. Tocqueville argued that in a very individualistic society such as the United States, religious sentiments still could turn people outward, put some moral brakes on individual striving, and remind people to care about others. It did not even matter if Americans fervently believed Christian precepts or not, he reasoned. If Americans expected of each other at least a lip-service faith in a good larger than their own private good, then they might keep alive a sense of connection to the wider society. Historically, faith-based groups in America sometimes have valued social togetherness beyond narrow interests and have cultivated that sensibility in the surrounding environment.[17] Is Tocqueville's optimism warranted today, when many Americans are sensitive to, and some are wary of, religion's public presence at all?

It is reasonable to think that Tocqueville could be right. The scriptures of both Christians and Jews contain potent images of communal cohesion, of care for strangers and the socially marginal.[18] Some of these images are familiar to religious people and religiously indifferent people alike; they are part of the American cultural mainstream. The Exodus story, for instance, is a story of shared revelation, shared fate, interdependence. It might be easy enough for contemporary religious volunteers or activists to draw metaphors from biblical images of communal cohesion: From African American slaves to white European colonists, Americans of all sorts have pictured themselves as latter-day Israelites, bound together as a community with a common fate.[19] Christians speak of the "Body of Christ"—a powerful image of shared responsibility to uphold Christian faith as an interdependent community. Jews and Christians also speak of a "covenant" with God, a collective obligation they must nurture.[20] Some contemporary religion scholarship argues that Christian faith offers theological resources for reaching out broadly to other members of society.[21]

Until fairly recently, sociological frameworks for studying religion tended to assume that any putative virtues of religion would work mostly privately, in the quiet of individual conscience, in the modern United States. There is some irony here, for on the empirical side, sociologists have had access to a long-standing, underappreciated tradition of community studies that depict religious congregations woven into the fabric of local public life in the United States, nurturing and sometimes threatening local ties.[22] Yet on the conceptual side, the "privatization thesis" that we introduced at the start tended to set social scientists' baseline thinking about religion in modern society until the late 1980s. Since that time, social scientists have been using other conceptual frameworks, including the civic lens, to accommodate different empirical findings on religion's public face—and to make sense of the fact that religion does indeed have many public faces in the contemporary United States.[23]

Some of these findings show us ordinary people carrying religion into local community life in ways that might confirm optimists' point of view. Students of faith-based community organizing conclude that religion sometimes can unite people for broadly public-spirited aims. They show how shared religious discourse and ritual help pastors, laypeople, and organizers to trust one another, and motivate one another, as they fight for better housing, new schools, and more control over urban development. These sociologists want to understand what enables grassroots, religious activists to win social justice battles and bring more low-income people into the political process at least temporarily. While they suggest some religious traditions are more effective than others in giving people the right resources for political thinking and political action, these scholars are optimists about the potential civic effects of at least some religion.[24]

Changes in social welfare policy, along with the continuing debate about America's civic health, are motivating more research on religious community service groups, partly to test out the optimistic claims of policymakers about the potential of "faith-based initiatives" in social service.[25] In the wake of welfare reform, researchers find that church-based groups are serving dinners at churches, distributing bags of groceries, "adopting" ex-welfare-receiving families.[26] Sometimes racial mistrust and denominational differences stall or preempt churches' efforts to collaborate in poverty-relief work, and church-based social service seems to cultivate "bonding" as much as "bridging" social capital.[27] Much more optimistically, one prominent survey of American congregations shows that these local institutions are impressive storehouses of social capital. They help to keep their own members from needing to seek governmental assistance, and they offer the larger society something more, too. "Norms" constitute one term in the troika by which Robert Putnam defined social capital, and many American churches cultivate a norm of civic engagement that would explain members' propensity to get involved better than would members' theological beliefs.[28]

Pessimists long have supposed that religion is a means to less virtuous or benign pursuits. For instance, Max Weber argued that for many Americans, being a part of the community—a full citizen, socially if not legally—often *depends on* maintaining membership in a congregation. Tocqueville might have agreed, but Weber's observation implies that for at least some Americans, membership in voluntary religious groups may be mainly a means to achieving a high social status, a privileged position in business relationships or social clubs.[29] Recent research on the public status of atheists suggests that at the very least, the moral status conferred by the social identity of "religious person" is still highly salient in most Americans' judgments of social worth.[30] A specific, shared religious identity also may help perpetuate "lifestyle enclaves" of people who feel safe and affirmed in each other's company and symbolically wall off a wider, messier public world.[31]

Other observers worry that religion too readily fragments public discussion and circumscribes the ties people can create. Given the continuing media fascination with "red" and "blue" states, and scholarly arguments about culture wars between religious conservatives and liberals, it is easy to assume that religion's influence on broad public debate usually is polarizing. Sociologists have been finding, though, that the "culture wars" framework for understanding American public opinion applies more to professional advocates and publicists than ordinary Americans—the focus of this book. Organizational and political interests may explain the shrill tone of religious publicists' arguments over abortion or lesbian and gay marriage as much as the force of faith itself. On this, proponents and opponents of the culture wars thesis might agree.[32]

Between optimists and pessimists, we find the optimistic tone to be dominant in recent studies that have moved beyond the creed of privatized religion in America. Each of this volume's contributors responds, implicitly if not explicitly, to this debate about American civic engagement. Broad overviews and select cases give us a nuanced look at what religious congregations and associations may, or may not, accomplish in the civic realm.

Beyond the Neo-Tocquevillian Celebration

We can study religion's civic life, its capacities and limits, just as we would study other kinds of associations. All of the chapters suggest that religious associations offer different combinations of goods and liabilities from those that other civic groups and traditions offer. Yet we can study those differences without assimilating some religious people's self-understanding that religious efforts are not "normal," that they come into the world from outside, in a pre-social, culture-free bubble.[33] We can also do so without assuming that religious languages and practices necessarily mark a privatizing, apolitical route toward the formation of insular communities. We do not propose that scholars are or should be indifferent to religion's place in civic life, nor that questions about religion never grow out of normative concerns for what a good society should be, whether secularist or religious. The suggestion simply is that we learn more when we assume neither that religion is "probably good for civic life most of the time" nor that it somehow diminishes civic life most of the time.

The chapters in this volume explore religion's civic life in just that spirit. They keep in mind the distinctive features of religious associations, rather than lumping churches, religiously based service alliances, or Christian social activist groups together with the Kiwanis Club or the League of Women Voters. Still, they help us understand religious associations in their capacity as civic actors. The essays take different, complementary approaches to civic life, focusing on its different facets—citizenly conversation, community building, volunteer social assistance, or social activism. Treating religious associations as participants in American civic life, the chapters ask questions we might ask of any civic group, such as how it does (or doesn't) facilitate mutual aid, cultivate relations with other groups, provide space for deliberating public issues, or produce potential resources, material as well as symbolic, for civic actors. Drawing on their own research projects, the authors represent a variety of methodological and theoretical approaches. Their chapters investigate the organizational, cultural, or geographical dimensions of religion's civic life, illuminating a variety of social forces, not simply reducible to theology or religious beliefs, that enable and constrain the actions of groups trying to act civically.

Michael Schudson's chapter on "The Varieties of Civic Experience" (Chapter 2) invites us to consider religious associations in a broader historical context. Observing that Americans have a long, varied history of civic participation, Schudson's chapter induces a healthy skepticism toward pat definitions of what "good" civic engagement could possibly be and what organizational forms it must take. The essay develops fresh reflections on some often-denigrated forms of associational life and challenges the popular notion that modern trends have weakened civic virtue. Schudson shows that those less-valued forms and supposedly harmful modern trends mark religious as well as secular associations today. His chapter is intended to make us think again about our own expectations regarding civic life, including the civic life of religion.

Nancy Ammerman (Chapter 3) bids us to consider U.S. congregations' internal imperatives as well as their distinctive, American institutional context if we want to understand how religious associations participate in civic life. On the internal side, she emphasizes that congregations need to sustain themselves as organizations with distinctively religious missions, quite apart from the other roles they may play in the wider world. Much of their efforts may be focused inward, yet congregations' internal community building creates nascent networks and alliances that become valuable during crises. On the external side, Ammerman explores the American institutional context that defines some of the internal imperatives of religious groups. She reflects on the fact that religious pluralism, denominationalism, religious strength, and legal disestablishment all create a need for religious groups to work at maintaining their own traditions on the one hand, yet be willing to coexist with very different religious groups. Consequently, congregations develop distinctive methods of connecting with other organizations, religious or secular. They combine religious work and public work in ways that are influenced by denomination (and politics) but do not map neatly onto "red versus blue" or simple theologically based divisions. Ammerman's chapter intends to leave us with good questions as much as firm answers in the current discussion over religion's civic potential.

Mark Chaves (Chapter 4) compares the amount of time and energy that American congregations put into three realms of activity: social service such as running a food pantry or homeless shelter staffed by volunteers, political educating or organizing, and the arts. Perhaps counterintuitively, Chaves finds that congregations spend more of their energies on arts than on the other two realms of activity that we more traditionally think of as having a civic impact. His chapter also investigates the relative importance of congregations' participation in these three big social realms, compared to all participation in those realms across American society, secular as well as congregation-based. Using material from his National Congregations Study, Chaves finds that congregations are most significant, again, in the realm of the arts rather than in the nationwide political or social service arenas. Like

Ammerman, Chaves suggests that the social organization of religion matters for its civic potential. He uses his findings to challenge the notion popular in some policymaking circles that congregations can become very significant alternatives to governmental social service agencies. Chaves's statistical overview of what congregations actually do primes us for considering congregations' civic activities more closely.

The organization of congregational life impacts congregations' interest in serving their immediate neighborhoods as well as the world at large. Omar McRoberts (Chapter 5) shows that the social organization of a "religious district" in Boston shapes and constrains the civic activity that is possible there. In urban spaces with a proliferation of small, "storefront" churches, the distances between congregations are more social and cultural than physical. Such congregations exist in highly fragmented civic environments, and their connections to the neighborhoods in which they reside can be very tenuous, or lived almost entirely in the realm of imagination: Different methods of carving out the boundary between the "church" and the "street" nurture or discourage civic connections in different ways. McRoberts's insights into the social geography of civic life suggest that the relationship between congregations and local communities is more complicated than popular understandings of the "helpful neighborhood church" suppose. The boundaries that religious groups navigate confer a certain moral status on those who fall within them, as well as on those who remain on the outside. If civic groups are, as some have argued, places where citizens learn to trust each other, McRoberts's findings also suggest that the contours of that trust are shaped by the symbolic worlds in which trust is generated.

The next two chapters pay close attention to the local practices and relationships that Chaves and Ammerman sketched with national samples. Studying two intercongregational alliances of the kind that Ammerman describes, Paul Lichterman's chapter (Chapter 6) situates the alliances in the broader U.S. institutional context, then examines religious deliberation—or its surprising paucity—in the alliances as members respond to changes in welfare law. Lichterman's essay demonstrates that building group identity and deliberating on public issues are very much intertwined tasks. Members of his two groups could do only as much religious deliberation as their group identity would allow, and that was not very much. Ironically, to be a "good" religious person necessitated not sounding too much like the widespread image of a religious person—someone who talks explicitly and at length about God's will. Though members did identify as religious, and though they held their beliefs strongly and sincerely, they understood the local public space as one in which sustained religious deliberation would be inappropriate. Ethnographic evidence from these two middle-American religious alliances challenges some popular arguments regarding Americans' purported affection for religious argumentation in public.

Dawne Moon's chapter (Chapter 7) investigates religious deliberation inside two congregations. In this case, her congregants were debating the inclusion of lesbian and gay people in United Methodist churches. Moon demonstrates how congregation members distanced their own positions from "politics," as they understood it, though they vigorously pursued the kind of thoughtful deliberation that scholars hope for in associational life. Congregants' arguments on both sides of the debate did not map easily onto progressive or traditional distinctions. Churchgoers on both sides took their ideas about what church is for to be nonnegotiable, distant from the negotiation and compromise that members disparaged as "politics" and that threatened to denaturalize deeply held religious convictions. If vibrant civic spaces nurture vigorous critical deliberation over common concerns, as normative visions of the civic often assume, Moon's chapter suggests in contrast that the civic spaces hosted by religious congregations are limited because the religious milieu encourages people to place certain topics out of bounds and often codes anything "political" as suspect.

Moving beyond Tocquevillian exuberance over religion's civic efficacy, the contributors are committed to treating religious associations as complex social formations. Schudson reminds us that the time between the writing of *Democracy in America* and today saw a great diversity of forms of civic life. Authors who take their cues primarily from Tocqueville miss much of what came before, and after, the vibrant associational life that he chronicles. They miss some of the civic potentials as well as liabilities in religiously based associations. In focusing on organizational realities, Chaves and Ammerman remind us that religious groups have to balance whatever civic work they do for a broader community with the work they do to maintain themselves as religious organizations in a society that makes religious participation voluntary. Normative hopes too often conjure up religious organizations as workshops of broad civic-mindedness, ignoring these organizational and institutional tensions. Lichterman and Moon both view culture and religious culture in more nuanced and empirically defensible terms than would the Tocquevillian who assumes that American religion in general acts as a bulwark against American individualism in general. Their studies show, too, that some of the implicit culture that matters in religious settings does not come directly from sacred texts but is potentially powerful nonetheless. Finally, McRoberts shows that delineating the boundaries of a community that matters for groups, and groups drain these boundaries in different ways Collectively, the authors demonstrate that even the most caring and committed members are hardly enough to make members' religious associations approximate normative ideals of civic inclusiveness, citizenly conversation, and concern for the greater good.

Chapter 8 returns to consider the questions raised in this and Schudson's chapter in light of other chapters' findings and suggests new directions for future research. We argue that new questions should be based neither on the assumption that individual moral virtue easily transforms into civic effectiveness nor on a knee-jerk cynicism that sees religious organizations as hopelessly naive or regressive. Instead, future research should be grounded by a more nuanced appreciation of what religiously based civic actors actually do in their social and institutional locations.

It would be premature at this point to pass a verdict in either direction on the civic potential of religious associations. Indeed, the chapters in this volume demonstrate that religious groups succeed and fail at their civic aims for a number of reasons that our commonsense notions of religion in American public life fail to appreciate. On balance the authors demonstrate that when religious groups are civic actors, their efforts often fail to live up to the high expectations set by political theorists and social critics, though not because religious actors are categorically unfit for civic projects. Instead, when religious groups fail in their civic aims, the reasons may have less to do with people's religious faithfulness than with the ways religious and nonreligious people create organizations in the United States. The sacred, in other words, may matter less than the mundane.

Notes

1. See Berger (1967), Luckmann (1967), and Parsons (1967).

2. While the literature is too broad to review here, for representative examples see Himmelstein (1989), Klatch (1987), Demerath and Williams (1992), Hart (2001), Smith (1996), Casanova (1994).

3. Membership in the Rotary Club, for example, is by invitation only, and prospective members must hold or have previously held positions in professional, military,

executive, or management positions; factory floor workers, retail clerks, or domestic workers are not eligible. This is not to say that such a group is "un-civic"; a certain degree of exclusivity is well within the bounds of what is usually considered normal in American civic life, though the trend in recent years has certainly been toward more inclusive membership policies.

4. See Kaufman (2002, 28–29).

5. For summaries of these trends, see Wuthnow (1994, 1998, 1999a); Smelser and Alexander (1999), Tarrow (1994), Skocpol (1999), and Putnam (2000).

6. For this definition, see Walzer (1992), Cohen and Arato (1992), Shils (1991), Wolfe (1989), Berger and Neuhaus (1977), and Etzioni (1996).

7. See Warner (1999) and Ammerman (1997).

8. See p. 66, and chapter 4 in general in Putnam (2000).

9. See Verba et al. (1995); Greeley (1997); Putnam (2000); Wuthnow, Hodgkinson, and Associates (1990); Eckstein (2001); Wilson and Musick (1997); Wilson (2000).

10. For recent studies that apply the "civic" lens to religiously based organizations, see, for example, Bartkowski and Regis (2003), Lichterman (2005), and Wood (2002).

11. See Tocqueville ([1835] 1969).

12. See Nancy Ammerman's chapter in this volume as well as her *Pillars of Faith: American Congregations and Their Partners* (2005).

13. See Mark E. Warren (2001). The most prominent tradition of inquiry into civic life, as Warren observes, is the Tocquevillian. A variety of viewpoints—liberal, communitarian, radical-democratic—have all drawn on aspects of Tocqueville's thought. There are still other traditions of inquiry into civic life: Learning both from Hegel and Marx's subversion of Hegel, the German critical tradition has kept alive its own hopes for civic groups, or civil society, to resist class domination and cultivate visions of a more just, more democratically driven society. See, for example, Habermas (1989), Cohen (1982), Cohen and Arato (1992). American sociologist Jeffrey Alexander (1993 [with Smith], 2001, 2006) has used Talcott Parsons's notion of the "societal community" to theorize the civic arena in a still different vein, emphasizing the conditions for justice and solidarity.

14. For these arguments, see Skocpol (1999), Wuthnow (1998), Bellah et al. (1996), Etzioni (1996), and Fukuyama (1999).

15. See Putnam's research (1995, 2000) on group memberships and his review of other studies of "social capital" and its outcomes. For a sharp review of some of the social capital literature, see Portes (1998).

16. For Putnam's own figures on declining memberships, see Putnam (1995, 1996, 2000). For the debate about those figures, see Cohen (1999), Edwards and Foley (1997), Wuthnow (1998), Fullinwider (1999), Greeley (1997), Schudson (1998), Skocpol (1996), Skocpol and Fiorina (1999), and Bellah et al. (1996). For accounts of Americans who

fear that community life is declining, see Wuthnow (1998), Wolfe (1989), and the fig-ures in Putnam (2000, 25). For a succinct review of the different strands of argument about social togetherness and civic decline, and some sober assessment, see Wuthnow (1999b). Worries about community are not new; for perceptive treatments of Ameri-cans' long-standing ambivalence about community see Hewitt (1989) and Bender (1978). Fears of communal decline are a staple of cultural criticism; see Lichterman (1996); see also Long (1984) and Bender (1978).

17. See Skocpol (1999); Casanova (1994); Demerath and Williams (1992); Wuth-now, Hodgkinson, and Associates (1990); McCarthy (1999).

18. On this point, see Fiorenza (1999) and Smith (1998), especially pp. 196–97.

19. See, for instance, Gorski (2000).

20. Apart from any specific teachings in the Judeo-Christian religions, a group that identifies itself explicitly as a religious group usually is one that nurtures a nonin-strumental, value-driven regard for other people. While much of modern life turns on strategizing, bargaining, impressing, or finessing, religious traditions still call people to care about society, about humankind, as ends in themselves. José Casanova (1994) elegantly argues that national religious leaders have become some of the most insis-tent, and least impeachable, proponents of the common good in modern societies; religious pronouncements against the nuclear arms race and economic injustice are two good examples.

21. See Gregory (2002), Mathewes (2002), and Mongoven (2002).

22. For representative studies, see Caplow et al. (1983), Douglass and de Brunner (1935), and Underwood (1957). For a contemporary example with a helpful overview of the tradition, see Demerath and Williams (1992).

23. For prominent statements of the privatization thesis, see Luckmann (1967) or Parsons (1967); see also Hammond (1992). For critical responses, see Regnerus and Smith (1998), Casanova (1994), and Chaves (1994).

24. See, for instance, Hart (2001), Mark R. Warren (2001), and Wood (2002).

25. For an exhaustive review of studies on faith-based social service groups and their effectiveness, see Wuthnow (2005). For conceptual overviews of contemporary faith-based coalitions or "special purpose" groups, see R. Stephen Warner (1999), Wuthnow (1988, 1999a), and Ammerman (1997), especially pp. 360–67. On mainline Protestants' public engagements, see Wuthnow and Evans (2002). For survey and in-terview findings on community involvement from national samples of congregations, see Ammerman (2002) and Chaves (2002).

26. See Bartkowski and Regis (2003) and Lichterman (2005).

27. Bartkowski and Regis (2003).

28. See Cnaan et al. (2002).

29. See Weber ([1946] 1974).

30. See Edgell, Gerteis, and Hartmann (2006).

31. See Robert Bellah et al. (1996). Sometimes those walls are physical, as in the case of suburban gated communities.

32. A number of scholars have argued that culture wars don't exist in the United States. See the extended argument in DiMaggio, Evans, and Bryson (1996). For the original statement of the culture wars argument, see Hunter (1991). Critics of the culture wars thesis have read Hunter's statement as claiming that there is widespread polarization among Americans. Hunter argued, and emphasized in a later book, that many Americans' private opinions are muddier, more ambivalent than the systematic, polarized public discourses he found, especially in the debate about abortion. See Hunter (1994).

33. See Orsi (1997).

Works Cited

Alexander, Jeffrey. 2001. "Theorizing the Modes of Incorporation: Assimilation, Hyphenation, and Multiculturalism as Varieties of Civic Participation." *Sociological Theory* 19:237–49.

———. 2006. *The Civil Sphere*. Oxford and New York: Oxford University Press.

Alexander, Jeffrey, and Philip Smith. 1993. "The Discourse of American Civil Society." *Theory and Society* 22:151–207.

Ammerman, Nancy. 1997. *Congregation and Community*. New Brunswick, NJ: Rutgers University Press.

———. 2002. "Connecting Mainline Protestant Churches with Public Life." In *The Quiet Hand of God*, Robert Wuthnow and John Evans, eds., 129–58. Berkeley: University of California Press.

———. 2005. *Pillars of Faith: American Congregations and Their Partners*. Berkeley: University of California Press.

Bartkowski, John, and Helen Regis. 2003. *Charitable Choices*. New York: New York University Press.

Bellah, Robert, Richard Madsen, William Sullivan, Ann Swidler, and Steven Tipton. 1996. *Habits of the Heart*. Updated edition with a new introduction. Berkeley: University of California Press.

Bender, Thomas. 1978. *Continuity and Social Change in America*. New Brunswick, NJ: Rutgers University Press.

Berger, Peter. 1967. *The Sacred Canopy: Elements of a Sociological Theory of Religion*. Garden City, NY: Doubleday.

Berger, Peter, and Richard Neuhaus. 1977. *To Empower People: From State to Civil Society*. Washington, DC: AEI Press.

Caplow, Theodore, Hoard Bahr, and Bruce Chadwick with Dwight Hoover, Laurence Martin, Joseph Tamney, and Margaret Holmes Williamson. 1983. *All Faithful*

People: Change and Continuity in Middletown's Religion. Minneapolis: University of Minnesota Press.

Casanova, José. 1994. *Public Religion in the Modern World*. Chicago: University of Chicago Press.

Chaves, Mark. 1994. "Secularization as Declining Religious Authority." *Social Forces* 72:749–75.

———. 2002. "Religious Variations in Public Presence: Evidence from the National Congregations Study." In *The Quiet Hand of God*, Robert Wuthnow and John Evans, eds., 108–28. Berkeley: University of California Press.

Cnaan, Ram, with Stephanie C. Boddie, Femida Handy, Caynor Yancey, and Richard Schneider. 2002. *The Invisible Caring Hand: American Congregations and the Provision of Welfare*. New York: New York University Press.

Cohen, Jean. 1982. *Class and Civil Society: The Limits of Marxian Critical Theory*. Amherst: University of Massachusetts Press.

———. 1999. "American Civil Society Talk." In *Civil Society, Democracy, and Civic Renewal*, R. Fullinwider, ed., 55–85. Lanham, MD: Rowman and Littlefield.

Cohen, Jean, and Andrew Arato. 1992. *Civil Society and Political Theory*. Cambridge, MA: MIT Press.

Demerath, Nicholas J., and Rhys Williams. 1992. *A Bridging of Faiths: Religion and Politics in a New England City*. Princeton, NJ: Princeton University Press.

DiMaggio, Paul, John Evans, and Bethany Bryson. 1996. "Have Americans' Social Attitudes Become More Polarized?" *American Journal of Sociology* 102:690–755.

Douglass, Paul, and Edmund de Brunner. 1935. *The Protestant Church as a Social Institution*. New York: Harper and Row.

Eckstein, Susan. 2001. "Community as Gift-Giving: Collectivistic Roots of Volunteerism." *American Sociological Review* 66:829–51.

Edgell, Penny, Joseph Gerteis, and Douglas Hartmann. 2006. "Atheists as 'Other': Moral Boundaries and Cultural Membership in American Society." *American Sociological Review* 71:211–34.

Edwards, Bob, and Michael Foley, eds. 1997. Special issue on "Social Capital, Civil Society, and Contemporary Democracy." *American Behavioral Scientist* 40.

Etzioni, Amitai. 1996. *The New Golden Rule*. New York: Basic Books.

Fiorenza, Francis. 1999. "Justice and Charity in Social Welfare." In *Who Will Provide? The Changing Role of Religion in American Social Welfare*, Mary Jo Bane, Brent Coffin, and Ronald Thiemann, eds., 73–96. Boulder, CO: Westview Press.

Fukuyama, Francis. 1999. *The Great Disruption: Human Nature and the Reconstitution of Social Order*. New York: Free Press.

Fullinwider, Robert. 1999. *Civil Society, Democracy, and Civic Renewal*. Lanham, MD: Rowman and Littlefield.

Gorski, Philip. 2000. "The Mosaic Moment: An Early Modernist Critique of Early Modernist Theories of Nationalism." *American Journal of Sociology* 105:1428–68.

Greeley, Andrew. 1997. "Coleman Revisited: Religious Structures as a Source of Social Capital." *American Behavioral Scientist* 40:587–94.

Gregory, Eric. 2002. "Augustine and the Ethics of Liberalism." Ph D diss., Department of Religious Studies, Yale University.

Habermas, Jurgen. 1989. *The Structural Transformation of the Public Sphere.* Cambridge, MA: MIT Press.

Hammond, Phillip. 1992. *Religion and Personal Autonomy: The Third Disestablishment.* Columbia: University of South Carolina Press.

Hart, Stephen. 2001. *Cultural Dilemmas of Progressive Politics.* Chicago: University of Chicago Press.

Hewitt, John. 1989. *Dilemmas of the American Self.* Philadelphia: Temple University Press.

Himmelstein, Jerome. 1989. *To the Right: The Transformation of American Conservatism.* Berkeley: University of California Press.

Hunter, James. 1991. *Culture Wars: The Struggle to Define America.* New York: Basic Books.

———. 1994. *Before the Shooting Begins: Searching for Democracy in America's Culture War.* New York: Free Press.

Kaufman, Jason. 2002. *For the Common Good? American Civic Life and the Golden Age of Fraternity.* New York: Oxford University Press.

Klatch, Rebecca. 1987. *Women of the New Right.* Philadelphia: Temple University Press.

Lichterman, Paul. 1996. *The Search for Political Community.* New York: Cambridge University Press.

———. 2005. *Elusive Togetherness.* Princeton, NJ: Princeton University Press.

Long, Elizabeth. 1984. *The American Dream and the Popular Novel.* New York: Routledge and Kegan Paul.

Luckmann, Thomas. 1967. *The Invisible Religion: The Problem of Religion in Modern Society.* New York: Macmillan.

Mathewes, Charles. 2002. *During the World: An Augustinian Theology of Public Life.* Book manuscript, Department of Religious Studies, University of Virginia.

McCarthy, Kathleen. 1999. "Religion, Philanthropy, and Political Culture." In *Civil Society, Democracy, and Civic Renewal*, R. Fullinwider, ed., 297–316. Lanham, MD: Rowman and Littlefield, 1999.

Mongoven, Ann. 2002. *Just Love: The Transformation of Civic Virtue.* Book manuscript in progress, Department of Religious Studies, Indiana University.

Orsi, Robert. 1997. "Everyday Miracles: The Study of Lived Religion." In *Lived Religion in America: Towards a History of Practice*, D. Hall, ed., 3–21. Princeton, NJ: Princeton University Press.

Parsons, Talcott. 1967. "Christianity and Modern Industrial Society." In *Sociological Theory and Modern Society*, 385–421. New York: The Free Press.

Portes, Alejandro. 1998. "Social Capital: Its Origins and Applications in Modern Sociology." *Annual Review of Sociology* 24:1–24.

Putnam, Robert. 1995. "Bowling Alone: America's Declining Social Capital." *Journal of Democracy* 6:65–78.

———. 1996. "The Strange Disappearance of Civic America." *American Prospect* 24.

———. 2000. *Bowling Alone*. New York: Simon and Schuster.

Regnerus, Mark, and Christian Smith. 1998. "Selective Deprivatization among American Religious Traditions: The Reversal of the Great Reversal." *Social Forces* 76:1347–72.

Schudson, Michael. 1998. *The Good Citizen*. New York: Martin Kessler Books.

Shils, Edward. 1991. "The Virtue of Civil Society." *Government and Opposition* 10:1–20.

Skocpol, Theda. 1996. "Unraveling from Above." *American Prospect* 25.

———. 1999. "Religion, Civil Society, and Social Provision in the United States." In *Who Will Provide? The Changing Role of Religion in American Social Welfare*, Mary Jo Bane, Brent Coffin, and Ronald Thiemann, eds., 21–50. Boulder, CO: Westview Press.

Skocpol, Theda, and Morris Fiorina. 1999. *Civic Engagement in American Democracy*. New York: Russell Sage Foundation.

Smelser, Neil, and Jeffrey Alexander. 1999. *Diversity and Its Discontents*. Princeton, NJ: Princeton University Press.

Smith, Christian. 1996. *Resisting Reagan: The U.S. Central America Peace Movement*. Chicago: University of Chicago Press.

———. 1998. *American Evangelism: Embattled and Thriving*. Chicago: University of Chicago Press.

Tarrow, Sydney. 1994. *Power in Movement*. New York: Cambridge University Press.

Tocqueville, Alexis de. [1835] 1969. *Democracy in America*. New York: Doubleday.

Underwood, Kenneth. 1957. *Protestant and Catholic*. Boston: Beacon Press.

Verba, Sidney, Kay Schlozman, and Henry Brady. 1995. *Voice and Equality: Civic Voluntarism in American Politics*. Cambridge, MA: Harvard University Press.

Walzer, Michael. 1992. "The Civil Society Argument." In *Dimensions of Radical Democracy*, Chantal Mouffe, ed., 89–107. London: Verso.

Warner, R. Stephen. 1999. "Changes in the Civic Role of Religion." In *Diversity and Its Discontents*, Neil Smelser and Jeffrey Alexander, eds., 229–43. Princeton, NJ: Princeton University Press.

Warren, Mark E. 2001. *Democracy and Association*. Princeton, NJ: Princeton University Press.

Warren, Mark R. 2001. *Dry Bones Rattling: Community Building to Revitalize American Democracy*. Princeton, NJ: Princeton University Press.

Weber, Max. [1946] 1974."The Protestant Sect and the Spirit of Capitalism." In *From Max Weber*, H. H. Gerth and C. Wright Mills, eds. New York: Oxford University Press.

Wilson, John. 2000. "Volunteering." *Annual Review of Sociology* 26:215–40.

Wilson, John, and Marc Musick. 1997. "Toward an Integrated Theory of Volunteering." *American Sociological Review* 62:694–713.

Wolfe, Alan. 1989. *Whose Keeper? Social Science and Moral Obligation*. Princeton, NJ: Princeton University Press.

Wood, Richard. 2002. *Faith in Action: Religion, Race and Democratic Organizing in America*. Chicago: University of Chicago Press.

Wuthnow, Robert. 1988. *The Restructuring of American Religion*. Princeton, NJ: Princeton University Press.

———. 1994. *Sharing the Journey*. New York: Free Press.

———. 1998. *Loose Connections*. Cambridge, MA: Harvard University Press.

———. 1999a. "Mobilizing Civic Engagement: The Changing Impact of Religious Involvement." In *Civic Engagement in American Democracy*, Theda Skocpol and Morris Fiorina, eds., 331–63. New York: Russell Sage Foundation.

———. 1999b. "Can Religion Revitalize Civil Society? An Institutional Perspective." Manuscript, Department of Sociology, Princeton University.

———. 2005. *Saving America? Faith-Based Services and the Future of Civil Society*. Princeton, NJ: Princeton University Press.

Wuthnow, Robert, and John Evans, eds. 2002. *The Quiet Hand of God*. Berkeley: University of California Press.

Wuthnow, Robert, Virginia Hodgkinson, and Associates. 1990. *Faith and Philanthropy in America*. San Francisco: Jossey-Bass.

2 The Varieties of Civic Experience

Michael Schudson

THE CONCEPT OF "THE CIVIC" IS so diffuse, and the activities one might plausibly regard as having an important civic dimension are so varied, that forms of civic engagement cannot reasonably be lined up and measured on a single scale of better and worse, more and less "civic." Nonetheless, many observers have taken this tack, including Robert Putnam and Theda Skocpol, the two distinguished scholars I will single out for special attention here. Both are concerned about the deterioration of older forms of civic life they believe more likely to achieve important public ends than newer forms of social activity that seem to be replacing them. I am reluctant to join in their critique because a look at the history of civic participation in the United States shows not only that *forms* of civic participation have changed but also that *ideals* of civic participation have been transformed. I suspect that Putnam, Skocpol, and others mourn civic practices in decline in part because they are captive of ideas and concepts affixed to and appropriate to a historical moment that has passed. What civic participation is best? That is too abstract a question. What forms are best will be relative to what forms are possible; what forms are possible will be relative to the historical and social conditions of a particular moment.

That is the claim I want to advance as I take a closer look at types of civic participation Putnam and Skocpol criticize. Their very standards of criticism arise from a set of assumptions pegged to the historical moment—now a memory—that generated the civic forms they believe most valuable. Without systematically reviewing Putnam's and Skocpol's work, I nonetheless will try to abstract from it the set of criteria they associate with ideal civic practices, and a set of characteristics they link to less effectively civic or un-civic activity. I will then make a case that there are many forms of legitimate civic and political activity today that bear the very features Putnam and Skocpol have disparaged, and that merit a more positive evaluation.

As for religious institutions as a locus of civic involvement, I will largely leave that topic to other contributors in this volume. The argument I make does not suppose that religious organizations share a characteristic style of civic engagement but that religious interest or affiliation in individuals and organized political engagement in religious institutions vary across religious groups, across time, and across circumstances of the moment. For instance, churches that today recruit and retain members by offering bingo nights or singles groups did not always do so. Evangelical congregations that once tended to eschew explicitly political stands and statements have in recent decades actively pursued partisan identification as a central part of their sense of purpose. Some churches may strongly encourage congregants to become politically or socially active and may provide information and organizational support for them to do so. In other instances, churchgoers judge anything "political" to be dirty and degrading and fear the entrance of political controversy into the church community itself as divisive and polluting—in recent years the church battles over homosexuality have aroused such concerns (Moon 2004, 123–46). Religiosity by itself or participation in a church under-specifies what civic engagement through the church might look like.

What sort of civic engagement is most honored has differed in different eras of American history. That is the main claim of my book *The Good Citizen* (1998). I cannot present the argument in full here. But a group of high school teachers suggested to me that my position is easily summarized if I restate my historical argument in terms appropriated from *The Simpsons*, the long-running popular television cartoon show. Even for readers who do not know the show, this may be clarifying.

In the United States, what contemporaries have honored as the ideal citizen or the normatively desirable citizen has differed across four eras, each of which can be represented by a different member of the Simpson family. The colonial era through the Washington and Adams administrations offers a model of "the deferential citizen." The ideal citizen in this era recognized the leaders of the community and voted for them, deferring on any specific issues to their judgment. Picture Marge Simpson, conscientious, moral, but normally knowing her place—deferential. In the 1700s, voter turnout was low, campaigning was discouraged, voters were supposed to measure candidates by their character and social standing, not their political ideas; voluntary organizations were welcome in private life but looked upon with suspicion if they ventured to offer opinions on public affairs.

In the early 1800s, as mass-based political parties emerged to replace the party-phobic world of the founders, the normative good citizen became not the deferential man of property but the democratic, enthusiastic (white male) partisan. This ideal is faithfully represented by Homer Simpson, including the fact that fellowship and partisan rivalry were often embraced for their own sake, regardless of issues or ideologies, and that the tavern's social life, not the party platform's intellectual life, was the center of political identification.

In that era, modes of civic participation multiplied as did the varieties of people welcomed as participants. The political party became the primary avenue of civic engagement. Parties involved masses of citizens in local and regional nominating conventions, and many more in the barbecues, picnics, torchlight processions, pole raisings, glee clubs, brass bands, hooliganism, and mass mobilization on election day. This festive politics proved remarkably sturdy and popular for most of the nineteenth century. Homer would have fit right in.

The period 1890 to 1920 brought a flock of important reforms, not matched anywhere else in the world, to assault party control and the enthusiastic mode of civic participation that it fostered. State-printed ballots replaced party-printed tickets; nonpartisan municipal elections in many cities supplanted party-based elections; the initiative, the referendum, and the direct election of senators sidestepped party machinery; and the growth of an independent commercial press replaced party-directed newspapers. All of these changes provided the institutional groundwork for an ideal of an informed, rather than blindly partisan, citizen. It is Lisa Simpson to a tee. This model of citizenship was well suited to single-issue and policy-oriented interest groups, from the Grand Army of the Republic and its advocacy of veterans' pensions to the women's suffrage movement. In fact, in the wake of the achievement of women's suffrage, the League of Women Voters emerged as a leading voice of information, informed policy discussion and debate, and a form of civic engagement determinedly at arm's length from party politics. Even the parties developed a more informational style of campaigning, moving from parades to pamphlets as they adopted what historian Michael McGerr (1986) terms an "educational" style of politics in the 1890s and after. The Progressive Era reforms did not destroy political parties, but the reformers, in their distaste for the nineteenth-century style of party politics, succeeded in promoting a new ideal of a rational, issue-centered, educated, and informed citizenry.

And Bart? What does Bart Simpson represent? Bart is the antiauthoritarian, individualist, irreverent, rights-claiming citizen of the era that the civil rights movement ushered in. It would be a mistake to see Bart as the anticitizen. Instead, he offers another ideal-type figure of what good citizenship can look like. To some degree, Bart just plays pure id to Lisa's pure superego, his impulse to her conscience, but that is not the whole story. Bart, like the representatives of so many of the liberation movements that have powered American politics since the civil rights movement, stands up for his rights, making aggressive and often self-serving claims. But to claim a right is not just to grab what you want; it is an implicit agreement to make a case on the basis of common principles, common aims, and common laws. Whether it is a pro-life or a pro-choice movement, environmentalism or advocacy for livable-wage ordinances, supporters of a patients' bill of rights or school choice, politics of the past half century has operated increasingly through mechanisms at the fringes of the parties and is not always readily linked to them. Historians do not yet know what to make of the bewildering array of political approaches these social movements have spawned, or the way they have enlarged—exploded—the arena of politics itself. In 1961 political scientist Robert Dahl observed that most people have little interest in politics; their primary activities are not politics but "food, sex, love, family, work, play, shelter, comfort, friendship, social esteem, and the like" (Dahl 1961, 279). It is easy to see that all of these topics (even, at least in California, "self-esteem") have been politicized. This is Bart's world, not entirely serious or sober or responsible, playful and brash and irreverent, sometimes charming and sometimes gross, breaking with convention, highly individualistic, and yet fueled by indignation at perceived injustice.

A question remains: Who or what does baby Maggie Simpson represent? What model of citizenship will she embody as she grows up? Consider this an open-ended question and not a matter of reclaiming some model from the past. The point of recounting this thumbnail history of changing American civic ideals is to lay the groundwork for the possibility that critics of contemporary American political life fail to recognize important forms of civic action because they are locked into past ideals of civic life, particularly the ideal of the "informed citizen." Different, and multiple, ideals of civic life undergird democracy. Recognizing each of them, and giving each its due, suggests a different valuation of a variety of contemporary civic or quasi-civic practices.

Robert Putnam and Theda Skocpol are two of our most systematic and thoroughgoing thinkers about what civic engagement today is and what it should be.[1] Neither is dogmatic about what counts as "civic." Nor are they peas in a pod. Where Putnam is concerned primarily with the vigor of associational life where people act on their own as the necessary condition for democracy, Skocpol is more interested in finding ways, particularly through governmental action, to remedy economic and social inequality that neither the market nor civil society handles effectively. Although sympathetic to each other's work, they have disagreements and have even sparred in print (Skocpol 1996; Putnam 1996). However, they share some assumptions about what the best, most generative, most effective, most lasting, most worthy forms of civic engagement are, and they do suggest along the way that some other forms are minimally civic or even counter-civic in their effects on public life. I want to make a case for a more pluralistic sense of what civic life should be and can be.

The Ideal Form of Civic Participation

Robert Putnam and Theda Skocpol have both argued that membership in national, cross-class, face-to-face chapter-based organizations has served the United States well as a foundation for civic life. Skocpol opens *Diminished Democracy* with observations on the gravestone of one William Warren Durgin of North Lovell, Maine. The headstone mentions not only Durgin's service as a Civil War veteran and pallbearer for Abraham Lincoln but also his membership in a veterans' organization (the Grand Army of the Republic), the Patrons of Husbandry or the Grange, and the Independent Order of Odd Fellows. As Skocpol wryly observes, however much she values her own active membership in the American Political Science Association and the Social Science History Association, she could not imagine herself requesting that "APSA" and "SSHA" be "chiseled into my gravestone" (2003, 5). Durgin's world of voluntary associations had a meaning and a weight that membership even in the same or similar organizations no longer carries. Skocpol expresses a longing for this world we have lost.

Why? What is so special about participation in groups like veterans' organizations, occupational associations, and fraternal orders? What makes these groups so civically admirable and effective is that they are (or were) simultaneously (1) grass roots, located in local communities and organized by chapters; (2) based on face-to-face meetings; (3) involving people often across lines of social class (like veterans' groups, at least for the World War II generation when military participation was broad and drew people from across classes more than it did in the Vietnam and Gulf wars); (4) oriented to fellow members across the country and to national legislative programs through affiliation with a national organization; (5) involving enough local social and charitable activity to engage a variety of participants in a variety of activities that generate social ties and social and political skills; (6) requiring people to commit time or energy; (7) depending little or not at all on paid, professional staff; (8) capable of generating moral and political demands on the state, especially on the national government; (9) providing an enduring organizational structure to ensure survival of the activity over time; and (10) operating by democratic election, rotation in office, and voting. In Skocpol's work, many of these characteristics are taken for granted. She does not write, for instance, of voting and elections inside the organizations she admires. In drawing attention to national organizations composed in federations of face-to-face, local chapters, she emphasizes the cross-class membership of participation in these organizations and their reliance on volunteer, lay leadership rather than professional staff.

In addition to these national voluntary organizations, I suspect Skocpol and Putnam would both recognize two other preferred models of civic engagement, the social movement and the political party. Social movements share many of the features of national chapter-based organizations, but they may not have an enduring organizational structure, they may be single-purpose rather than multidimensional in their activities, they may or may not bring people together across class or across other major social divides, and they are likely to require greater time commitment than the national chapter-based organizations. They are also likely to be more centrally defined by (1) asking participants to take significant risks of time, energy, and public visibility and vulnerability; (2) asking participants to present themselves as oppositional to some aspect of the going state of affairs; and (3) asking participants to define their involvement in terms of moral concerns and moral claims on state power.

As for the political party, in the United States it has typically been a cross-class and cross-region alliance, but whether it has demanded face-to-face time-consuming participation has varied over U.S. history and, at present, is much weaker than it was in the nineteenth and early twentieth centuries for lack of such participation. Still, the orientation of parties to national policy, the vestigial importance of grassroots participation, the ultimate dependence of the parties on at least a momentary act of mass participation on election day, the harnessing of moral fervor to the needs of national policy, and the maintenance of an enduring organizational structure to recruit and renew public participation all bring to the parties at least some of the ideal features that Putnam and Skocpol see in the veterans' organizations or the PTA.

What kinds of organizations are left out when you pull together the features of parties, social movements, and national chapter-based organizations as vehicles of good civic behavior? At least the following are omitted and are explicitly or implicitly disparaged in the work of Putnam, Skocpol, and others:

- Groups that are oriented to goals too particular, local, and self-serving; there is disparagement of NIMBY (Not In My Back Yard) groups that define the public good (if they define it at all!) in terms of highly localized self-interested needs. (Putnam mentions NIMBYism as evidence that groups that generate social capital may be committed to "malevolent, antisocial purposes" [2000, 22].)
- Groups that emerge around momentary crises or events that fail to generate sustaining social capital. (Putnam compares marches on Washington of the 1990s unfavorably to those of the late 1960s because the more recent marches were not "preceded and followed by continuing activism in communities across the country" and offered "no assurance of continuing, community-based action" [2000, 164].)
- Groups that are driven by the views and values of paid professional staff where public participation is too easy and too cheap to generate either social capital or individual commitment from members. Skocpol writes critically of the shift she has seen since the 1970s from "membership to management" in American civic life when "new social movements and professionally managed civic organizations took to the field in huge numbers, redefining the

goals and modalities of national civic life" (2003, 219). This has built a society that is "still a nation of organizers but much less a nation of joiners, because civic leaders were no longer committed to mobilizing vast numbers of fellow citizens into ongoing membership activities" (2003, 220). Skocpol argues that we should recognize the downside of "professionally managed, top-down civic endeavors" that in the end diminish democracy (2003, 232).

- Non-group, individual activity, particularly of ornery or evidently self-interested individuals and their advocates in the legal system, often obstructionist rather than solidaristic like the atheists or the American Civil Liberties Union in pursuing relatively trivial dimensions of the separation of church and state. Putnam sees the growing number of lawyers since the 1970s as a sign of "the fraying of our social fabric" as Americans turn to formal institutions and the law to resolve conflicts that social trust and social networks once managed quite well (2000, 147).

- Groups that are more therapeutically oriented than politically oriented and have an explicitly or implicitly antipolitical stance, seeing hope for the future not in collective solutions but in self-responsibility or person-to-person caring, familial rather than political. Putnam's data indicate that self-help groups are the only kinds of organizations or associations people belong to where membership is not positively correlated with "voting, volunteering, giving to charity, working on community problems, or talking with neighbors" (2000, 151).

For Putnam and Skocpol (and in this they are representative of many academics and social critics who worry about a broad decline of civic spirit), forms of civic participation can be disparaged if they are (1) oriented to private interests or personal transformation rather than public purposes; (2) transitory, occasional, or event-centered rather than enduring in mobilizing and maintaining public participation; (3) individual rather than collective in civic strategy; and (4) cheap and convenient for participants rather than demanding of risk, sacrifice, or investment of time and energy.

You may believe that I am barking up the wrong tree if I am now about to sing the praises of episodic organizations, NIMBY organizations, litigious cranks, and twelve-step groups. Well, I am not making an argument *against* national chapter-based organizations, social movements, or political parties. But these kinds of organizations should not exhaust our civic imaginations. Other forms of participation have a place that should be recognized and perhaps honored, not disparaged. They should be honored and their advantages exploited because, first, they suit the individualistic and pluralistic society that we have increasingly become; and second, they are in fact capable of generating social connection, civic benefit, and moral claims upon the state.

One might go further with the following supposition: The kinds of national chapter-based organizations Putnam and Skocpol favor—and this includes churches—will do better under present social conditions if they seek to recruit and retain members through an emphasis on personal transformation, a willingness to exploit event-centered activities, attention to individual-based strategies of civic purpose, and adaptation to forms of involvement that are relatively convenient and safe for people to try. Are such strategies lacking in virtue? That is a judgment I am not prepared to affirm—these are strategies that may bind individuals to the church while coaxing them to a public purpose in tune with the church's spiritual aspirations. In fact, this seems to be exactly what clergy and lay leaders in the churches have themselves concluded—they have been running ahead of, not behind, the theorists of civic life.

Insufficient Orientation to Public Purposes: Therapeutic Groups and NIMBYs

In Robert Putnam's remarkable body of data on the perilous decline of civic participation since the 1960s, he finds several countertrends, among them a significant growth in self-help and support groups, from Alcoholics Anonymous to Weight Watchers. He accepts that support groups provide many members improved health and psychological well-being. They are especially valuable for people who are most isolated from other social networks; divorced and single people participate at much higher rates than married people. To their credit, Putnam concludes, many support groups "bring problems hitherto dealt with in isolation into a communal forum" (2000, 151). They turn private troubles into social relations, and sometimes (although not often) they are organized in a way to pursue directly political goals. Mothers Against Drunk Driving and the Association for Retarded Citizens have both acted directly in the public and legislative realm.

Even so, for Putnam, support groups fail to provide what the old-style civic associations did so well. Membership in self-help groups is not correlated with other community involvement, from voting to volunteering to talking with neighbors. The groups are not families. They are not communities. Their connection to a larger public life is "sometimes tenuous and hard to detect" (2000, 152).

I accept Putnam's characterizations but not his conclusions. No one claims that support groups are the best way or the only way to organize our social life. A twelve-step group is too inward-looking and, besides, it deals with the individual tragedies and sorrows of life, cancer or addiction or obesity or compulsive gambling—things not essentially about the distribution of power and privilege but about the distribution of fortune. In this sense, support groups are probably more like churches than they are like the PTA. What they lack, that churches have often provided, is a full-service program of activities—people can join the church because they want solace in grief or a preschool for their children or a safe and congenial social setting for expressing spirituality, for finding a mate, making friends, or drumming up clients for a business. Whatever the reason may be, the church provides them entrée into a wide variety of activities, some of them civic.

This is more rarely the case with therapy groups, although it does happen. Some of the 9/11 families came together initially as emotional support groups, to be able to grieve together. As these groups consolidated, they morphed into advocacy groups, and it is widely acknowledged that their efforts were decisive in forcing the Bush administration to agree to an independent 9/11 investigating commission. It is likewise clear that pressure from these groups forced Condoleezza Rice to testify before the commission. Hundreds of family members have joined in nearly one hundred lawsuits seeking damages from defendants as varied as Osama Bin Laden, the government of Saudi Arabia, and the New York Port Authority.[2]

But surely this is the exception, not the rule. What may be more important with support groups is that sometimes they work. That is, sometimes they provide individuals insight, strength, and support. They make better, stronger individuals. These people may be in a position to help others who suffer from similar ills. They may be understanding of their family and friends and coworkers in ways they were not before. They may find themselves more able to cope with the world and more ready, even, to respond to opportunities for civic engagement. Putnam's data indicate they do not vote more, give more to charity, or talk more to their neighbors. It may be that therapy groups offer less a mode of civic engagement than a collective and democratized mode of medical practice. If they contribute to civic health, they may do so primarily by contributing to individual health. They do so in a way that is antiorganizational, antibureaucratic, and antiprofessional. When they succeed, the participant eventually ceases to be a participant and exits from the group (and from Putnam's measures of membership), but then, healthier, more autonomous, and more convinced of the power of the kindness of strangers, they may choose civic engagement. They may not. I do not know of evidence one way or the other.

All of this discussion presumes—mistakenly—that civic organizations and support groups are different species. In fact, therapy groups and support groups of various kinds are frequently sponsored by the sorts of organizations that Putnam recognizes to be good incubators of civic activity: churches. Robert Wuthnow even identifies inside conventional churches the growth in recent decades of what he calls "the small-group movement" that he judges to be "effecting a quiet revolution in American society" (1994, 2). Wuthnow's national survey found that 40 percent of Americans belong to a "small group that meets regularly and provides caring and support for its members" (1994, 4). Many of the groups, drawing on models of small-group interaction from medicine, therapeutic communities, social psychology, and group dynamics, were also modeled on 1960s ideas of democratic engagement, self-expression, and knowledge as something constructed rather than something handed down by a tradition or an authority. Importantly, Wuthnow observes that it was often clergy and lay religious leaders who introduced small groups in their churches, convinced that traditional forms of community inside the church were not serving the needs for community and belonging or drawing out the spirituality of members (1994, 43).

To the extent, then, that churches remain unusually strong locations for civic engagement in American society (compared to most other industrial societies), it is difficult to argue that this is a trend entirely separate from therapy groups; they have become intertwined. The churches have adapted to the individualistic ethos of modern American life and modern religiosity by providing the small-group expressive, communal, and quasi-therapeutic rewards that seem so much more congenial to baby boomers (and younger generations) than to their parents.

A case can be made for the civic value of NIMBY groups, too. Two of the more effective neologisms of the past quarter century are *NIMBY* and *NIMBYism*.

We seem to accept that NIMBYism is a bad thing, but the history of the term is instructive. William Safire (1993) traces its first use to the American Nuclear Society, the trade association of the nuclear power industry. The term came into general use particularly among critics of environmentalists in the early 1980s and especially critics of those who protested the siting of hazardous waste disposal in their neighborhoods. Until the mid-1970s, siting decisions had been left to market forces and the private decisions of petrochemical corporations. Although twenty-five states had some relevant legislation, the Environmental Protection Agency reported to Congress in 1974 that in practice hazardous wastes "are essentially unregulated" because none of the states had fully implemented its laws. As for the federal government, a comprehensive program to regulate the treatment and disposal of hazardous waste emerged only with the 1976 Resource Conservation and Recovery Act (Szasz 1994, 11). It was only with the emergence of an environmental movement in the 1960s and 1970s and the passage of key environmental legislation that government bureaucrats came to play a role. The large-scale social ramifications of land use became more apparent to many, and state governments took on powers and established agencies authorized to override local decisions.

In this context of a growing role for democratic decision making in land use, the NIMBY phenomenon appears. It accompanies growing democracy, it is made possible by growing democracy, and of course it has been fueled by growing distrust of science and expertise.[3] NIMBY sentiment has blocked the siting of hazardous waste disposal facilities, halfway houses, the release and placement of sex offenders in residential neighborhoods, and so on. I do not suggest that this has always been to the greater good or that NIMBY conflicts are ideal forms of deliberation. I do suggest that NIMBY groups have not only mobilized people for civic engagement but that they have done so in the name of the democratic process and they have been empowered by forms of democratic review and accountability that simply did not exist before the late 1970s. They do not displace a prior world of rationality or democracy but a world of private, corporate decision making.[4]

NIMBY organizations have some Lisa Simpsons in them. On the environmental scene, NIMBY groups have sometimes become experts in scientific and technical matters, able to debate corporate or government scientists cogently. But they have more than a little of Bart Simpson in their brash disrespect for politics as usual, their unwillingness to defer to established authorities, their sometimes histrionic, publicity-seeking ways of operating. Because they are so committed to democratic processes and public contestation, I am unwilling to conclude that they are insufficiently oriented to the public good. They may, however, be insufficiently enduring.

Insufficiently Enduring Civic Participation

The infrastructure of experience today may give unusual aid and comfort to political activity organized around events and occasions rather than around institutionalized groups. Consider the argument, made by political scientist Bruce Bimber, that the growth of what he calls "postbureaucratic" organizations offers a new capacity for "speed, opportunism, and event-driven political organization" (Bimber 2003, 192). Some organizations, through careful targeting of subpopulations of the general public, have been able to mobilize people far beyond their own membership lists for specific political actions. In fact, this has been successful enough to effectively change what these organizations even mean by "membership." Membership changes, in a sense, "from issue to issue and event to event. As information grows more abundant, the boundaries and membership of a political organization are increasingly a function of the particular event in which it is involved" (2003, 209).

Bimber does not expect the digital era of political communication to stimulate an increase in civic participation (2003, 228). He is not a starry-eyed Internet utopian. He recalls that it was not the generally competent and serious Howard Dean in 2004 who was the first politician to benefit from Internet-generated fund-raising but the naive populist Jesse Ventura in his successful 1998 campaign for governor of Minnesota. But Bimber does expect that the vastly increased access to political information that the Internet provides to millions of people will alter the character of the public sphere. He points to the Million Mom March of May 2000 as a case where a massive mobilization of people emerged entirely outside of conventional civic and political organizations. One person, unaffiliated with any groups, conceived the idea, and as late as September 1999, her organization consisted of one phone line and two volunteers.

Was the Million Mom March a political success? It did not get Congress to pass the gun control legislation the organizers sought—but then, conventional political pressures have also failed to achieve gun control legislation. It did not establish an enduring organization. It did, however, raise $2 million, bring tens of thousands of people with little or no prior political experience to a march in Washington, and win extensive media attention.

How important are such flares of political activity if they do not give rise to sustainable political organization? How important are they if the character of contemporary life makes them more and more possible and more and more successful in their own limited terms? Is it true that temporary, transitory, and occasional events are not well suited to building enduring social ties or political skills? I once shared this view. Serving on a committee that distributes small grants to San Diego community groups, I joined with my fellow committee members to deny support for proposals to stage onetime cultural events like an annual neighborhood picnic or fair. I now think that was the wrong decision. Sometimes putting a festival together builds social capital. It requires planning, committee work, deliberation, vision, imagination, and compromise. It may even be self-consciously oriented to serve "political" ends. This is the case, for instance, in the revival or invented tradition of "Day of the Dead."

Communication scholar Regina Marchi (2005) has found that Day of the Dead rituals in the United States contain political and cultural significance absent in their original Latin American setting. She notes that Day of the Dead festivities transcend divides of class and ethnicity in the Latino community as well as divides between immigrants and people whose families have been in the United States for generations. In Oceanside, California, the chamber of commerce initiated a city-wide Day of the Dead event for the most mundane and self-interested of reasons: The Chamber wanted more visitors in downtown Oceanside and sought to transform the image of a city sometimes regarded as hostile to ethnic minorities.

Once begun, the project had multiple community-building consequences. Recent immigrants, with the most knowledge of the "authentic" rituals, took charge and became the tutors and teachers for second-, third-, and fourth-generation American Latinos and for non-Latinos. People came to know one another and develop skills at working together and bridging social divides. "There are lots of meetings," one volunteer told Marchi. "So we have business people, artists, Mixtec people, designers, teachers all working together.... There's people who speak Spanish and people who speak English and people who speak Mixtec or Zapotec. ... We had the Boy Scouts and Girl Scouts involved. ... On the day of the event, everyone is working together. ... People who know about Day of the Dead and those who didn't know about it before all work together." And this is just the beginning. As Marchi shows, Day of the Dead events not only bring Latinos together but also generate understanding and appreciation of Latino culture among others who come to enjoy the Day of the Dead celebration as participants in the planning or as observers and tourists at the scene. Furthermore, as the events come to be widely recognized in the general culture, political activists take full advantage. Immigrant rights activists in recent years, across the United States, have sponsored Day of the Dead processions and altars critical of U.S. border policies.

Churches have long maintained an effective event-centered orientation; Christian churches are packed on Christmas and Easter while the assembled congregation is much thinner on an ordinary Sunday, despite the ministry's best efforts to insist that no Sunday is ordinary. But congregations may devote more attention to special events than they once did, and at least some prominent organizations that Alan Wolfe (2003) dubs "parachurches" revolve around rare, massive assemblies. Wolfe discusses Promise Keepers, a national organization that began in the early 1990s to encourage men—not women—to renew and revivify their Christian faith through attendance at mass rallies held in football stadiums and other large sports venues. Even conventional churches, in an age of widespread spiritual seeking and weakened attachment to the church one grew up in, may be relying more on the occasional carnival, cruise, retreat, potluck, or golf tournament to market themselves to their own members or to encourage the interest of nonmembers.

In our informational system today, in our present politics of ethnic and other identities, with our present media hungry to cover events, event-centered, transitory, but effectual organizing may be a growing part of civic life that has more potential for sustainability than is apparent on the surface.[5]

Insufficiently Collective Civic Participation

Few features of contemporary life are more disparaged by the critics of declining civic engagement than American individualism, particularly that of baby boomers and the generations that have followed them. The boomers, as Putnam has observed, "vote less, campaign less, attend political meetings less, contribute less, and in general avoid their civic duties more than other generations" (2000, 258). They also marry late and divorce often, leave the religion in which they were raised and rarely return to it, are less loyal to a particular company or workplace, and are "more insistent on autonomy." They are more libertarian and more tolerant than their parents, less respectful of "authority, religion, and patriotism." They are "highly individualistic, more comfortable on their own than on a team, more comfortable with values than with rules." And all of this has been socially harmful because these people volunteer less, give less, trust less, and provide "less shared responsibility for community life" (2000, 258–59).

At the same time, the result of all of this is not what, in a European context, Putnam calls *incivisme*. This is what Putnam found in an earlier study in some regions of Italy where there is little involvement in associational life and where most people see public affairs as "somebody else's business," that of bosses or politicians. People feel powerless, exploited, unhappy. But this is clearly *not* the American situation. The American brand of individualism may be privatizing, may weaken traditional civic associations and political actions, but it is not antithetical to political involvement. It is not necessarily linked to a sense of powerlessness. There are a variety of individualistic approaches to political action that cannot be easily dismissed.

Some critics have seen people's preoccupation with individual rights as a particularly American feature of the civic problem. Instead of seeking to work out common solutions to problems, people rely on untrumpable claims on the state or the public that they call "rights." This looks, to some critics, like an extreme individualism, almost an atomism, that wreaks havoc with social trust and social connection. But rights are anything but individualistic. They exist in practice only when governments are prepared to enforce them. This happens only when governments are willing to invest resources in courts, police services, and offices full of lawyers willing to take a matter to court on behalf of a citizen or a group of citizens. All of this, as Stephen Holmes and Cass Sunstein have argued, costs money. Money requires taxation. Rights are not simply a claim of individuals against the state but a claim of individuals that the state itself underwrites for the good of all. This includes property rights of individuals that Holmes and Sunstein (1999) judge "an indispensable condition for democratic citizenship." For them, a decentralized economy including property rights that government cannot confiscate at its whim provides "a reliable material basis for an unintimidated political opposition" (1999, 196). Rights are not possessions of individuals against the government; they are "powers granted by the political community" (1999, 17).

It is today a familiar observation that the worst thing for the cause of women's liberty to make decisions about their own bodies was the Supreme Court decision in *Roe v. Wade* to legalize broad accessibility to abortion. Some proponents of pro-choice politics have held that, in retrospect, taking a judicial route to abortion access was in the end a terrible error in judgment. It won a right but it did not win broad public support. We are now instructed that seeking to legitimate same-sex marriage through the courts rather than the legislatures is producing, just as *Roe v. Wade* did, a passionate backlash. But how does the political seer of the rearview mirror figure out when people should give up their right to pursue justice in the legal system and when they should exercise that right? Did the NAACP make a political error in seeking school desegregation in the 1940s and 1950s through the courts? Should the NAACP have taken the slower, tougher, but more lasting stance through the electoral process? It is hard to imagine recommending such a choice.

Antipathy to strategies that use the courtroom for political ends is one underlying theme in contemporary American discussions of civic engagement. Everybody loves to hate a lawyer. But we should not be too quick to jump on this bandwagon, especially when, as one harsh critic of contemporary tort law writes, class action suits offer "the new town meeting" of political participation (Huber 1988, 83). This goes much too far, but it does suggest that there is a collective, politicized dimension to civil litigation.

The capacity of individual citizens to raise a ruckus by suing powerful corporations has become a significant political force. The tobacco industry was under attack for years before it was dealt its most severe (although not crippling) blow. This came not from legislators and not from the surgeon general but from a set of individual attorneys and finally state attorneys general seeking damages for individual citizens or the families of individual citizens who had suffered disease or death from tobacco addiction. Individual litigants made a difference, too, in the efforts to gain reparations from corporations that worked with and for the Nazi government in Germany. A handful of Holocaust survivors, aided by platoons of lawyers, brought to their knees the Swiss banks that had profited by supporting Hitler's regime. While a handful of survivors led the charge, some twenty thousand of them were in the end able to share in a payout of more than a billion dollars.

Suing private corporations for damages to achieve political ends is largely a product of the past half century, spurred by new rules governing class action suits and inspired by the successes of litigation strategies in the civil rights movement and its successor movements for the rights of women, gays and lesbians, people with disabilities, and others. Few individuals have the economic resources to sustain a long courtroom battle, but if the prospects are good for a large settlement, the costs of litigation will be borne by a small set of public-interest or economically motivated contingency-fee lawyers. Litigation for school desegregation, courtroom battles for gay and lesbian rights, and litigation challenging the tobacco companies all have stimulated public awareness, public education, and political organizing.

Some of these rights-based struggles have torn apart traditional civic organizations, including churches. The civil rights movement challenged labor unions and private clubs that discriminated against African Americans; it railed against other groups, too, including even liberal churches, as Martin Luther King Jr.'s famous letter from the Birmingham jail suggests. The women's movement assaulted business clubs and professional organizations that excluded or demeaned women while criticizing churches that denied women ordination. Today churches are torn asunder by battles over the morality of homosexuality and by lawsuits against clergy for child sexual abuse, another issue that is a product of the individualistic, rights-based style of civic participation. It may be that some organizations and some churches will arise strengthened by these conflicts; others will lose the loyalty of their members—and, many would add, that is just what they deserve.

Civic Activity Insufficiently Demanding of Risk and Sacrifice

In the eyes of critics, some of the forms of political engagement I am seeking to validate here are just not sweaty enough. If you don't look like Charlie Chaplin on the assembly line in *Modern Times*, you aren't doing politics right. Civic engagement should hurt. It should be uncomfortable. Writing a check to the Sierra Club doesn't count. Complaining about surly, inefficient, or negligent service from school, government, or corporation isn't civic engagement at all, it's just complaining. Moral posturing is easy, as Allan Bloom observed in criticizing the rebel morality of the 1960s. For him, morality should be not "histrionic" but humble, exercised in daily acts of telling the truth or paying one's debts—and this morality "always requires sacrifice" (Bloom 1987, 325).[6] This seems to be the assumption of both conservative critics and left-wing critics of contemporary American civic morality—that we do not have much of it, or, to the extent that we do, it is a morality of the easy way out.

This does not do justice to current civic life. It ignores how much event-centered civic activity gives rise to intensely energetic efforts for limited periods of time—whether this is the weeks of organizing for the Day of the Dead or whether it is the tens of thousands of Americans who serve time after time as election day clerks or the tens of thousands who raise money for breast cancer research and treatment in a twenty-six-mile walk or whether it is the Million Mom March. Even more, it omits altogether consideration of two domains whose civic activity requires—in very different ways—plenty of sweat. One, ironically, is the increase in the number and percentage of people whose civic engagement comes from a life's commitment to full-time work in the public or nonprofit sectors. When Skocpol looks to organized civic groups, she is seeking to locate volunteer activity beyond the workplace or the family. Nowhere do the dour accounts of Putnam and Skocpol make allowances for the increase in the number of people whose *jobs* are oriented to public service. To the extent that Skocpol deals with it, she sees it as a negative factor—the more that professionals take on the operation of public service organizations, the less of a role there is for the rank and file. A figure that strikes me as important and positive—that today there are an estimated eighteen million people or 8 percent of the U.S. labor force doing human service work in nonprofits—Skocpol cites as unhappy evidence that we have moved from a membership to a management society. (And she fails to note that this figure represents a great increase, with the number of human service organizations themselves having increased from 300,000 in 1967 to 1.4 million in 1992.)[7]

Professionalization, for Skocpol, is a danger to civic life. For her, if political parties are run not by volunteer precinct workers but by jet-set media consultants and pollsters, the whole activity of party politics becomes just another domain of professionally managed human activity and not the central self-governing act of democracy. But even if we might want to concede this for politics, as a special and important case, it is unlikely that we would also want to criticize the school system for having taken on the professional management of children's education or hospitals for having professionalized home health care or social service agencies for having displaced neighbors, grandmothers, and peer groups in offering counseling, occupational therapy, hot meals for the homeless, and so forth. Is there a social cost to every one of these changes? Yes, Skocpol is right to call it to our attention. But the social gain is substantial, too, and it is difficult to imagine turning back this clock.

This is not to say that the benefit of professionalized social services derives necessarily from public-oriented civic virtues. A person may choose to be a schoolteacher or a clerk in the Social Security office for reasons that have little or nothing to do with a sense of civic duty. There is no reason to assume that a teacher is a better human being than an insurance salesman; you can't read virtue off of a job card. But some jobs in themselves require civic service constantly—and there are more such jobs in total and as a percentage of all jobs than there used to be. The professionals working for nonprofits recruit a vast army of volunteers. Volunteering an occasional hour or even a regular hour or two on a weekly or monthly basis is something an increasing number of Americans have been doing in the past decades. They do it because they are high school or college students who may get course credit for it or gold stars from fraternities or sororities or other clubs they belong to. They do it because they are secure enough and healthy enough in their retirement to want to give back to the broader community. They do it because they want to be engaged—but in a structured way with a controllable commitment of hours. And they do it because the growing army of nonprofit organizations asks for their help. One of the reasons the nonprofit professional/volunteer relationship has flourished is that more and more people see community problems as "extremely serious." The old-style club woman and good neighbor who worked on an after-school program or a library addition were likely to see their work as charitable but not likely to view it as wrapped up in earth-shaking public issues. Volunteers today are more likely to recognize that their efforts are directly or indirectly tied to problems of racism, inequality, homelessness, and other serious ills (Wuthnow 1998, 46–47).

The second form of civic engagement that is highly demanding of risk and sacrifice but largely ignored by social critics is highly individual, highly expressive, or therapeutic in orientation, but intensely risk-taking. What I have in mind are various political acts on the domestic scene—the woman who leaves her partner for a women's shelter or who seeks a restraining order against him, say; the teenager who comes out gay to his family and friends. Granted, the woman who seeks refuge in the battered women's shelter is not doing the same sort of civic act as the volunteer who helps at the shelter or the professional who manages the shelter or the philanthropist who funds it. The young people who bravely come out are not performing the same civic act as the people who organize the gay pride parade or who go to court to win domestic partner benefits or who lobby for same-sex marriage laws. But they are still taking the step of recognizing a private trouble as a socially or politically organized trouble to which there might be social or institutionalized remedies.

Risk-taking for the public good takes on a variety of highly personal and individualistic forms. Political theorist Nancy Rosenblum (1999) lists two personal "dispositions" she finds particularly important for building a democratic society. First, she mentions the inclination to treat all people equally and informally, a kind of democratic spirit in manners, an easy openness to all people equally and without standing on ceremony. Second, she mentions the willingness to speak up over small, everyday injustices, a disposition that draws on an insistent sense of right and wrong and a willingness to intervene, even across the chance of embarrassment or conflict. For her, this kind of speaking up is most vital in the most inconspicuous moments, the moments of everyday life when one may choose, for instance, to break a polite silence to say something about a racist or sexist remark one has just heard or overheard, or to break a polite inattention to intervene when an older child cheats or bullies a younger one, or when a clerk speaks rudely to a customer—or a customer to a clerk.

I would add to Rosenblum's list another democratic disposition: frankness. A growing frankness in public discourse spurs and is spurred by a growing frankness in everyday talk. Much of this frankness is about intimate life, sexual, medical, or otherwise. It was a moment of considerable social importance in 1974 when Betty Ford, First Lady in the White House, publicly acknowledged that she had undergone surgery for breast cancer. Her frankness prompted tens of thousands of women to get cancer screenings who would not otherwise have done so. A few years later Mrs. Ford would pioneer in revealing publicly her addiction to alcohol and prescription drugs.[8]

Of course, contemporary frankness may be self-indulgent, solipsistic, or simply vulgar in rock music lyrics or TV or radio talk shows or contentious political rhetoric. Even this, for all of its crudeness, has been part of an opening over the past half century that has transformed what it is possible or safe for people to discuss in their daily lives. (Old-fashioned virtues of discretion and civility have their own appalling consequences in hypocrisy, self-righteousness, and the various indignities and repressions of the silent, repressed, and unspoken.) The expansion in the past half century of what counts as political to include aspects of intimate life, health, and sexuality, but more broadly bringing the lives of women and children into public discourse, has been on balance a boon for men and women, adults and children.

Talking about politics as such is not easily done. Politics is a dangerous and divisive subject today as in the past. People's own native tact and eagerness to maintain sociability, preventing their own or their social partners' embarrassment, screens out or skirts around political topics even in our putatively frank era and even, as Nina Eliasoph (1998) has shown, in avowedly civic or political groups. This reticence has scarcely disappeared. Even so, supported by a wider culture, people take up topics in everyday talk today they could not have imagined discussing with their friends or family or coworkers a generation ago.

Conclusion

Many scholars and activists intent on improving civic participation in our country, and deeply worried by signs of the degradation of civic life in declining voter turnout and declining membership in many of the civic organizations that served society in the 1940s, 1950s, and 1960s, have arrived at a view of what counts or what should count as "public life" or "civic engagement" that is too narrow. Using the work of Robert Putnam and Theda Skocpol, two of the most imaginative, ambitious, and substantial of these thinkers, I have tried to extract a set of features of organized civic activity they admire and, by implication or express statement in their work, a set of features of quasi-civic or pseudo-civic or un-civic organized activity they disparage. This exercise led to the identification of four kinds of activity Putnam and Skocpol find wanting—activity not sufficiently oriented to the public good, not sufficiently enduring and institutionalized, too individualistic, or lacking in a commitment of time, energy, or risk. In each of these instances, a closer look leads to a different conclusion—that apparently privatized or transitory or individualistic or apparently low-cost actions may have far-reaching civic benefits.

Nostalgia for old forms may be almost inescapable, but the effort to get past nostalgia is vital. We must be able to register not just how society closes off access to once-thriving forms of group life but opens avenues to others. I am not thinking here of technological changes like the Internet, although in the past ten years that has become a factor in civic participation as in so much else. I am thinking more of social changes in family, work, and kinship. I am thinking of broad demographic changes from the rapid increase in single-person households to the rapid rise in the prevalence of and legitimacy of divorce; of broad changes in the labor market, including the dramatic rise in women's paid employment in the labor force. We live in a period of rapid growth of higher education that privileges professional accomplishment more than volunteer amateurism and critical acumen over adherence to dogma; and in a culture of individual autonomy that saw in 1955 only 4 percent of Americans practicing a religious faith other than the one they were born into—a figure that rose to 33 percent by 1985 (Wuthnow 1988, 88–89). I am thinking of all these phenomena that social scientists and historians have not yet been able to piece together into a comprehensive portrait of the underpinnings of any kind of civic participation in the present age. If we do not recognize the depth of these changes, their enduring importance, and, for that matter, the extent to which they represent what are arguably advances for human freedom and equality, it will be difficult to know what kinds of civic engagement today are possible, or desirable, or even to determine what civic engagement means.

Some of the American founding fathers who lived into the early nineteenth century looked with horror at the new social forms emerging in that era. What, they wondered, had happened to the civility that had been so essential to the formation of a new republic? Why were the selfless men who stood for office in those first years being replaced by self-seeking organization men of that upstart and obnoxious organizational form, the political party? It might be very well for more people to participate more actively through these new forms, but the cost to sensible, civil, and peaceable government could throw the country into ruin! The aging founders who made these arguments were right to see value in the earlier era and to see that some of it would be lost forever. But they were wrong, too—wrong for failing to recognize that the gross and rude new forms embodied virtues of their own, virtues better suited to a shifting social order than the founders' preferred set of civic dispositions could ever be.

Notes

This chapter was first published in Michael Schudson, "The Varieties of Civic Experience," *Citizenship Studies* 10, no. 5 (January 11, 2006): 591–606. Reprinted by permission of the publisher (Taylor & Francis Ltd., http://www.tandf.co.uk/journals).

1. Their contributions are many but I will be focusing primarily on Putnam's *Bowling Alone* (2000) and Skocpol's *Diminished Democracy* (2003).

2. See Jim Dwyer's "Families Forced a Rare Look at Government Secrecy," *New York Times*, July 22, 2004, A14. On Saudi Arabia's response to lawsuits filed against the country on behalf of the 9/11 families, see *Newsweek*, April 16, 2003, reported on the MSNBC Web site www.msnbc.msn.com/id/3067906/.

3. On this point, see Mazmanian and Morell (1990).

4. See, for instance, Munton (1996).

5. This leaves aside the argument that transitory occasions of communal sentiment that happen *without organizing* are also of political and social consequence. I

have in mind claims about the moral significance of spontaneous gatherings in the wake of widely noted and deeply felt mass-mediated experiences like the death of Princess Diana. See Roseneil (2001) and, for a fuller sociological treatment of similar phenomena, Katz and Dayan (1992).

6. One knows exactly what Bloom means, on the right, and what Putnam and Skocpol mean, on the left. But I think they are all seeking to engender individual morality and not civic engagement.

7. See Skocpol (2003, 214). The data is from Robert Wuthnow's *Loose Connections* (1998, 47).

8. See Greene (2004). The rise of public frankness since 1960 is the topic of my present research.

Works Cited

Bimber, Bruce. 2003. *Information and American Democracy*. Cambridge: Cambridge University Press.

Bloom, Allan. 1987. *The Closing of the American Mind*. New York: Simon & Schuster.

Dahl, Robert. 1961. *Who Governs?* New Haven, CT: Yale University Press.

Eliasoph, Nina. 1998. *Avoiding Politics: How Americans Produce Apathy in Everyday Life*. Cambridge: Cambridge University Press.

Greene, John Robert. 2004. *Betty Ford: Candor and Courage in the White House*. Lawrence: University Press of Kansas.

Holmes, Stephen, and Cass R. Sunstein. 1999. *The Cost of Rights*. New York: W. W. Norton.

Huber, Peter. 1988. *Liability*. New York: Basic Books.

Katz, Elihu, and Daniel Dayan. 1992. *Media Events: The Live Broadcasting of History*. Cambridge, MA: Harvard University Press.

Marchi, Regina. 2005. "Altar Images: US Day of the Dead as Political Communication." Ph D diss., University of California, San Diego.

Mazmanian, Daniel, and David Morell. 1990. "The 'NIMBY' Syndrome: Facility Siting and the Failure of Democratic Discourse." In *Environmental Policy in the 1990s: Toward a New Agenda*, Norman J. Vig and Michael E. Kraft, eds., 125–44. Washington, DC: CQ Press.

McGerr, Michael. 1986. *The Decline of Popular Politics*. New York: Oxford University Press.

Moon, Dawne. 2004. *God, Sex, and Politics*. Chicago: University of Chicago Press.

Munton, Don, ed. 1996. *Hazardous Waste Siting and Democratic Choice*. Washington, DC: Georgetown University Press.

Putnam, Robert. 1996. "Robert Putnam Responds." *The American Prospect* 25:26–28.

————. 2000. *Bowling Alone: The Collapse and Revival of American Community.* New York: Simon & Schuster.

Rosenblum, Nancy. 1999. "Navigating Pluralism: The Democracy of Everyday Life (and Where It Is Learned)." In *Citizen Competence and Democratic Institutions,* Stephen L. Elkin and Karol E. Soltan, eds., 67–92. University Park: Pennsylvania State University Press.

Roseneil, Sasha. 2001. "A Moment of Moral Remaking: The Death of Diana, Princess of Wales." In *Culture and Politics in the Information Age: A New Politics?,* Frank Webster, ed., 96–114. London: Routledge.

Safire, William. 1993. *Safire's New Political Dictionary.* New York: Random House.

Schudson, Michael. 1998. *The Good Citizen: A History of American Civic Life.* New York: Free Press.

Skocpol, Theda. 1996. "Unravelling from Above." *The American Prospect* 25:20–25.

————. 2003. *Diminished Democracy.* Norman: University of Oklahoma Press.

Szasz, Andrew. 1994. *EcoPopulism: Toxic Waste and the Movement for Environmental Justice.* Minneapolis: University of Minnesota Press.

Wolfe, Alan. 2003. *The Transformation of American Religion.* Chicago: University of Chicago Press.

Wuthnow, Robert. 1988. *The Restructuring of American Religion.* Princeton, NJ: Princeton University Press.

————. 1994. *Sharing the Journey.* New York: Free Press.

————. 1998. *Loose Connections: Joining Together in America's Fragmented Communities.* Princeton, NJ: Princeton University Press.

3 Building Religious Communities, Building the Common Good: A Skeptical Appreciation

Nancy Ammerman

FOR MANY PEOPLE, CITIZENS AND THEORISTS alike, "religion and civic life" seems like a contradiction in terms. A long tradition of theorizing in the social sciences associates religion with traditionalist and/or nonrational ways of life, often equating religion with the sort of single-minded commitment to truth that precludes the give-and-take civic life requires.[1] As Stanley Fish put it in a *New York Times* editorial column, "The truth claims of a religion—at least of religions like Christianity, Judaism and Islam—are not incidental to its identity; they are its identity. . . . Religion's truth claims don't want your respect. They want your belief and, finally, your soul. They are jealous claims" (Fish 2007). Fish doesn't want schools to teach about religion, and one can only imagine what he would think about the possibility of a civic conversation in which religious actors and religious claims were present. A long tradition in U.S. culture declares that "religion" is one of those things that should not be discussed in public. Civic spaces, it is thought, should be not just religiously neutral but utterly devoid of religion, lest civility itself be lost.[2] For many who take that view, the recent prominence of combative religious conservatives is vivid proof that crossing the religion-politics divide is a mistake.

Against that backdrop, a more recent body of literature has sought to show the positive contributions of religion and religious organizations to public life (Smidt 2003). Some advocates seem almost convinced that civil society is impossible *without* religion. Picking up themes first articulated by George Washington, they claim that "of all the dispositions and habits, which lead to political prosperity, Religion and Morality are indispensable supports. In vain would that man claim the tribute of Patriotism, who should labor to subvert these great pillars of human happiness, these firmest props of the duties of Men and Citizens" (Washington [1796] 2007). These enthusiasts for the role of religion in establishing a necessary morality are joined by a chorus of policymakers who argue that religious organizations are the society's best hope for delivering social services, as well as for forming good citizens (Sherman 2000; Cnaan 1999).

Somewhere between those two extremes lies the much more interesting question of *how* religion intersects with civic life. Even those who fervently believe that it shouldn't, nevertheless realize that it does. And those who are convinced that it must, realize that it often does not. Religious organizations in the United States are active in civic and political life. They are not the only players, but they are present. A wide range of religiously based public interest groups routinely seek to educate both their own members and the larger public on policies as diverse as welfare reform and foreign policy, and local congregations often provide a space in which conversations about public issues take place (Wuthnow and Evans 2002). When people gather religiously, they often speak and act in ways that address the meaning of being a community of citizens. The question here is not should or shouldn't. The questions are whether, under what circumstances, and with what effect. As Casanova argued, there is a crucial distinction between wielding state power and exercising public influence (Casanova 1994). The U.S. Constitution has forbidden the former but allowed wide leeway for the latter.

After a decade of studying congregations in the United States, including thinking about how they differ from religious gatherings elsewhere, what follows is an account of what I've observed, suggesting that neither utter faith in the civic virtue of religion nor utter skepticism is in order. In addition, I want to outline some of the questions that remain unanswered—hinted at in the data we have, but not yet fully understood.

The U.S. Context

It is important to begin with an understanding of the particular political, historical, and legal context in which this conversation is happening. That context is shaped by two important realities: legal disestablishment and the relative strength of religion in U.S. culture. Religious ideas, symbols, and organizations have a cultural salience here that demands they be taken into account. Almost all Americans say they believe in some sort of God, at least most of the time. For three-quarters of them, it is a personal God, and 64 percent say they depend on this God for strength and support in times of crisis. Only 22 percent will venture to say that faith in God isn't very important to them. While the terms *religious* and *spiritual* are highly contentious, and even some strong believers reject them, 61 percent of American adults say they are at least moderately religious, and 62 percent say they are at least moderately spiritual.[3] A substantial portion of the American population, then, claims some sort of personal relationship with a God they value, especially in the hard times. While people may not always overtly acknowledge their religious leanings, they can and sometimes do, knowing that there is a good likelihood that others around them will share some version of those leanings. Even people who have become religious "nones" (expressing no religious "preference") usually are believers of some sort (Hout and Fischer 2002).

In a nation where religious beliefs are so prevalent, it is perhaps not surprising that religious rhetoric is also ubiquitous in political discourse. To a degree that scandalizes many Europeans, public officials in the United States seem to end nearly every speech with some equivalent of "God bless America," and solemn state occasions often call forth nationalist theologizing. The "civil religion" of the United States incorporates motifs from Jewish and Christian scriptures (Bellah 1963), but at its most basic, American conversation about what it means to be a citizen is likely to include a sense that the nation's religious heritage is part of its strength. The persistent collective mistrust of those without beliefs (Edgell, Gerteis, and Hartmann 2006) reinforces the assessment that religion and civic life are, for good or ill, historically intertwined in the United States.

Not only is some form of individual belief widely present in U.S. society, organized congregations and denominations persist in large numbers and wide variety as well. While only a quarter of the population are among the most devoted who attend every week (and sometimes more than once a week), almost that many more claim to be present at least once a month. This is the population from whom Gallup regularly measures something on the order of 40–45 percent "weekly" attendance. Not all of that 40 percent was probably present on the Sunday in question, but as regular attenders most weeks, they routinely tell Gallup interviewers what they think should have been an accurate answer even when it isn't (Hadaway, Marler, and Chaves 1993). The point is that about half of American adults have a fairly serious habit of attending religious services. Another quarter show up once or a few times a year, while the last quarter attend rarely, if ever.

The places they attend represent a remarkable diversity of religious traditions, and that is one result of the second key factor framing our understanding: disestablishment. Law and society in the United States have created a space for voluntary religious communities, and believers of all sorts have taken advantage of that free space. The range of belief and practice in U.S. culture is greater today than ever before, but diversity has been a fundamental fact of our form of religious organization nearly from the beginning (Hatch 1989; Butler 1990; Greeley 1972). Pluralism is, as Stephen Warner puts it, "constitutive" of American religion (Warner 1993).

In spite of this religious diversity, U.S. history has seen remarkably little religious conflict, especially of the violent sort. When a firebomb strikes a synagogue or a mosque, it makes news, and the community surrounding the group often rallies to express its outrage. Violence is certainly not unknown, but neither is it a routine way of life. In spite of the fact that dozens of religious groups would argue that they and they alone have the true way to live, disestablishment means that no one of them has the power to coerce obedience (Demerath 2001). When the "Standing Order" was abolished in Massachusetts and the state constitution was amended in 1833, the last vestige of state-sponsored religion ended. Limiting the ability of religious groups to use state power to enforce religious boundaries of citizenship has meant that each new group of arrivals has had to transform whatever expectations they may have brought with them into practices of civic participation that fit the limited power available to religious groups in the U.S. "denominational" system (Handy 1972; Mead 1963). Here all groups are (seemingly) equally powerless.

They are also equally required to fend for themselves. Not only could they not expect the state to enforce their way of life, they could also not expect the state to help them perpetuate it, even among those already within the fold. The denominational system requires as well as permits. It permits free exercise, but requires each group to spend its own organizational energy creating communities in which to worship, educate young and old, and care for each other's worldly needs. The implication for religious groups themselves was that they would have to learn to be one among many and to take responsibility for their own well-being. That is what it means to be a "denomination." When we recognize a group as part of a denomination, we expect both a measure of distinctiveness and a willingness to play by U.S. rules of tolerance (Ammerman 2005a, chapter 7). Religious groups can celebrate their own unique identity, but they must also recognize the limits of their power. That's the basic legal and cultural system within which any conversation about civic engagement takes place.

Balancing Bonds and Bridges

That legacy involves, then, both the commitment to live alongside others and the willingness to invest voluntary resources in preserving and extending one's own traditions. The Constitution guarantees the right to gather into religious communities, but it does not guarantee that any given group will succeed in its efforts. Only the group's own voluntary energies can do that, and this is a point at which interests in civic engagement may seem to clash with the interests of faith communities themselves. If religious groups are to sustain their distinctive way of life, they have to engage in the work of worship, religious education, and fellowship among their own members.[4] They have to spend most of their organizational energy on creating a store of religiously based "bonding capital" (Putnam 2000). All of their connections and conversations are concentrated within the group, and they invoke divine sanctions on the line between their way of life and the evil outside world. Such bonding capital can lead to insular communities that respond to civic life and cultural diversity in hostile and unhelpful ways. Religiously sanctioned racism, anti-Semitism, and nationalism come to mind, with "Christian Identity" movements being perhaps the most extreme example (Aho 1990).[5] Sometimes the benefits of a group's bonding redound only to its own members, generating corresponding costs for those deemed "other."

Tightly bonded gatherings of religious compatriots can sometimes bode ill for the well-being of the larger community, but we will not understand why and how so long as we assume *either* that all religious gathering is civically virtuous or that all religious gathering is inherently fractious. We need tools for understanding the vast space between those two poles. Religious groups can, for instance, spend most of their energy building internal relationships and condemning outsiders and still be concerned with where they fit in the larger civic scheme of things. What they say about outsiders may not directly predict actual hostile relationships. Even groups that spend a great deal of time patrolling their symbolic borders may, as Smith shows in his study of evangelicals, have workable rules for engaging those on the outside (Smith 1998).

Most American religious groups, however, promote a discourse of acceptance and tolerance more than a discourse of exclusion (Wolfe 2003). And most of the worry about bonding capital is about its less-virulent versions. The point often made about religious groups is not so much that they actively hate outsiders as that they divert their members' attention toward comfortable (even otherworldly) activities and away from the complicated world of strangers and public difficulties. All our studies of congregations show, for instance, that they spend far more of their time on worship than on public debate, far more time teaching the faith to their own children than teaching reading to others, far more time having fellowship potlucks than feeding the hungry in the community (Chaves 2004). The organizational energy of congregations goes primarily into the religious and spiritual work that is their primary reason for being (Ammerman 2005a). Lichterman and others are absolutely right to emphasize that congregations are primarily about generating spiritual and social goods for their own members (see Chapter 1 of this volume). I would suggest, then, that understanding how religious communities contribute to civic life requires that we start by understanding how they do their religious work, looking for the unintended consequences as well as the intended ones.

We might note, for instance, that there is a good deal of evidence suggesting that the bonding capital congregations generate can and does, under many conditions, enhance civic life. That evidence, however, does not always make clear just what the mechanisms for this effect are. While we can draw out correlations between religious participation and civic participation, that relationship may or may not be the result of explicit teaching or any other direct intention on the part of the religious group. In fact, it is pretty clear that most religious communities, most of the time, pay no attention at all to matters of civic concern. So what is happening in what at first appears to be "merely" religious space?

Congregational Life and Civic Practices

Sometimes, of course, congregations do attempt to bring civic life directly into their circle of concern. We would do well to start our inquiry by listening to what they have to say about what they and their members ought to be doing in the world. The specific theological and moral teachings of religious traditions do matter. But listening to their discourse about the world will require that we go beyond assumptions about which religious traditions are or are not "activist" or "this-worldly." Far more useful are close readings of local religious cultures and individual religious worldviews. Recent research that has begun to do this sort of exploration provides considerable complication to any neat "otherworldly/red-church versus this-worldly/blue-church" map. Thirty years ago, it was commonly assumed that evangelicals were disengaged from public life, while liberals were more likely to be involved in community social services and political activities. Groups with the most "otherworldly" aims and/or the most stringent lifestyle demands were thought to find civic engagement an unwanted competitor for member commitment.[6] The growth of the New Christian Right and the emergence of evangelicals into the middle-class suburban mainstream of U.S. society have combined to erode that earlier expectation of quietism (Smith 2000). Similarly, "liberal" Protestants and Catholics are often less socially active or politically liberal than earlier expectations might have predicted. Whatever it is that connects religious life with public life is not easily measured by liberal versus conservative or this-worldly versus otherworldly theologies.

I have argued elsewhere that we do better by asking how people say they should live. In doing so, I have identified three recognizable bundles of practices that orient the actions of U.S. Christians—evangelical practices, activist practices, and Golden Rule practices (Ammerman 1997, 2005b). Most interesting for the current discussion is the "Golden Rule" orientation. Golden Rule Christians say that the most important virtues are practicing "Christian values" in everyday life, taking care of those who are sick or needy, and sharing what they have with those less fortunate.[7] This orientation is toward individual caring and benevolent (if sometimes condescending) community service. Churches, in this view, should promote a strong sense of fellowship for their own members, but also provide aid and services to people in need. Some religious traditions encourage these practices more than others, but people with a Golden Rule orientation are found across the theological spectrum. And wherever they are found, higher levels of volunteering and community service are found as well. This orientation is by far the majority position among American churchgoers, suggesting that it is a Golden Rule morality that is most often taught to those who participate. In the context of a local religious community, they are shaped in a world of rhetoric and practice that values "love of neighbor."

It seems to me worth continuing to unpack how religious ideas and practices are intertwined with ideas and practices related to public life. My own explorations suggest that religious ideas about engagement in the larger community interact in complicated ways with other aspects of religious and everyday life (Ammerman 2005b). People in religious communities engage in civic life based in part on their stage in life, economic conditions, ethnic traditions, and a host of other factors. Nor is civic engagement a unitary reality. How religious communities enact the connections varies from praying for public officials to writing letters of protest, from carrying a saint through the public streets to organizing a forum on youth violence or opening a food pantry. Even when we are listening for explicit ideas and stories about how religious life and community life relate to each other, there will always be "modifiers" on both those terms.

Indeed, we would also do well to leave open the question of how religious and civic action are intertwined. Ziad Munson's work is a welcome reminder, for instance, that religion and politics are often indistinguishable in the practices of activists. When they enact their public concerns, they do it with practices that are at once spiritually charged and politically strategic. Symbols and experiences are thoroughly infused with both realities (Munson 2006).

But what about non-activists and indirect consequences? What about the practices that are "simply" religious or "simply" about internal bonding? Are there indirect ways in which those practices nevertheless matter for communities beyond the congregation itself? What kinds of conversations and ideas may be generated inside religious communities that help members interpret for themselves what it means to be civically engaged? What might members be taking with them from one arena to another—a sense of agency, of calling, of compassion? And exactly where do they take those things? Do religious symbols and practices end up in other social spaces?

We have known for some time, for instance, that congregations seem to be pretty effective at inspiring people to volunteer, but we are just beginning to understand how they do it. We know that members are more likely to volunteer than nonmembers, and deeper involvement in the life of the congregation pays off in deeper involvement in service to the larger community. In research on Christian congregations, I found that when people do more than come just for an occasional service, they are more likely to be involved in both informal caring and organized volunteering in the larger community. Across all the Christian denominations, participants who are most involved outside the congregation are also those who are most active in the church itself.[8] Far from taking people *out* of the community, active participation in church fellowship, education, and mission groups makes them more likely to get involved in other works of service as well. Sheer involvement with fellow parishioners in the give-and-take of church life seems to provide increased opportunity to invest in the well-being of others, within and beyond the church's membership.

Research on mobilization for immigrant rights, especially the huge public demonstrations of spring 2006, provides an interesting window on how congregations encourage civic engagement. March participants interviewed in Chicago were exceptionally likely to be Catholic and to attend services frequently. They didn't come to the march from church (it wasn't Sunday, after all) or say that someone at church persuaded them to come (most claimed that *no one* "persuaded" them to come), but their parishes had been full of information about the upcoming events, and priests strongly encouraged participation. Not all parishes are pro-immigrant or politically active, but a solid core of Chicago parishes had created religious communities in which concern for human rights and full engagement in citizenship were part of the culture (Davis, Martinez, and Warner 2007).

This contrasts with more typical Catholic parishes, which are not always so good at nurturing "civic skills." Across traditions, both practices of caring and practices of collective decision making are "portable," but not all congregations cultivate these skills equally. Verba, Schlozman, and Brady (1995, 328–30) highlight, for instance, the opportunities for leadership (and therefore enhanced civic skills) experienced especially by the least-well-off religious participants. Experience gained in internally focused activities such as organizing youth socials or moderating a church council meeting can spill over into civic and political life. Where people have congregation-based opportunities to organize and lead, they often carry those skills with them into civic and political participation. Verba et al. make the point, however, that religious traditions (e.g., Protestant versus Catholic modes of authority) do make a difference, either enabling or constraining action. That is, the routines of decision making in congregational life do vary from tradition to tradition, and those variations affect how and whether religious participation indirectly affects civic life. A big, anonymous, top-down religious organization simply doesn't encourage the civic engagement that a moderately sized, egalitarian one does (Bane 2005). Both ideas and social structures make a difference.

Another of the indirect links between congregation and community is the network of relationships within and beyond the religious community. Paxton reports, for instance, that members of religious groups are especially likely to be members of other voluntary organizations, and such "connected" membership is especially beneficial for sustaining democracy (Paxton 2002). The civic work of congregations varies, then, depending on the breadth and character of the networks to which they connect their members. My own research found that virtually all congregations had at least one tie to a local charitable organization, sending money, providing space and other resources, as well as sending teams of volunteers.[9] These interorganizational connections are part of what makes congregational participation a potential bridge to individual community engagement. A variety of earlier studies have noted that volunteerism is facilitated by network ties that provide information, normative sanction, and relational bridges—all mechanisms likely to be present in congregations (Becker and Dhingra 2001; Park and Smith 2000). One of the best predictors of community involvement is simply whether or not one has been asked (Musick, Wilson, and Bynum 2000), and congregational relationships and activities seem to be prime settings in which such asking takes place. In addition, when problems are too big to be solved by volunteering, congregations are also often the seedbed out of which new religious and civic organizations grow (Milofsky and Hunter 1995).

Congregations themselves are strategically engaged in civic concerns largely through the partnerships they form. Most are simply not big enough to have much impact on their own, so they seek out others with whom to pool resources. They participate in informal coalitions, contribute to religious and secular nonprofit agencies, and even form alliances with businesses and governmental organizations. The question is not whether congregations will work in partnership, but what kind of partnerships they will nurture. The bridging potential of those partnerships often goes unrealized because the networks are more nascent than active. Volunteers are sent off in multiple directions, perhaps inspired by their religious tradition, but are rarely afforded opportunities to bring together the world they serve and the world where they worship. Small groups of activists carry the organizing load and rarely speak of their work to their fellow parishioners (Lichterman 2005).

Sometimes it takes a disaster to unsettle the routines and activate the implicit links. When riots struck Los Angeles in 1992, for instance, congregations became a primary organizing point for recovery. That was possible because they were already present in the community, but also because they were already linked to denominations and other organizations that mobilized volunteers and resources (Orr et al. 1994). A disruption activated nascent connections. After September 11, 2001, similar mobilization of nascent networks occurred, opening up spaces for public conversation and connection, as well as for the delivery of essential social services (Ammerman 2002). Volunteers from the whole range of religious communities found themselves working together to respond to disaster.

But what about when there is no visible disaster? What patterns of organization and interaction more and less effectively link the experiences of congregation activists with the rest of the members? What ongoing relationships are more and less effectively mobilizable? How do routine patterns create and sustain latent networks? Are there paths from some kinds of congregations into specific sectors of public life, while other kinds of congregations connect people elsewhere? Future work needs to explore these mechanisms more thoroughly. What kinds of interactions and conversations, in what kinds of settings, are creating (or inhibiting) bridges between congregational life and different forms of community engagement? Building bridges is not easy. Wuthnow's work suggests, for instance, that members who volunteer are consistently more likely to have friendships that cross social class lines (Wuthnow 2003). But are cross-status relationships essential to public life? Lichterman tells us that the picture is complicated by the way a group talks about its relationship with those it serves (Lichterman 2006). Groups may or may not create verbal pictures of a world in which they and those they serve share a common civic domain. Simply counting numbers of volunteers or numbers of programs is not enough to provide a robust picture of the discursive worlds created by religious communities. It is in those worlds that we are most likely to glimpse the practices and meanings that structure the civic life of religion.

Congregations and Politics

Careful listening to religious communities at work will also help us to see how they construct their role in the political domains of civic life. Wuthnow provides a detailed picture of how much political activity and of what sorts we might find in congregations of various religious traditions, but he notes that hearing a sermon about poverty, for instance, may or may not tell us how and why members participate in political life (Wuthnow 2002). Sermons, in fact, may be the most contentious and least effective form of civic and political discourse in congregational life. Smith's interviews with individual evangelicals suggest that most do think they should be involved in the political process, but they don't like their pastors preaching about politics (Smith 2000). Churchgoers in general (at least white ones) seem not to like their churches taking up issues that are likely to evoke "political" (i.e., contentious) conversation (Moon 2004).

Some congregations are involved in political activity, however, with different religious traditions adopting different strategies: Catholics tend to organize demonstrations and lobby; African American Protestants offer political opportunities to their members, discuss politics, have speakers, and register voters; mainline Protestants discuss politics and have speakers; while evangelicals are the most likely to hand out conservative voter guides (Beyerlein and Chaves 2003). Given the intense focus of recent Republican campaigns on using wedge issues to mobilize conservative churches, those guides may be creating an increasingly solid and polarized voting bloc. Still, the question of mobilizing religious communities is a difficult one. Both the logistics of making connections to more than three hundred thousand local organizations and the illegality of direct partisan activity make it likely that most political activity will be ad hoc and indirect.

What none of these studies yet addresses, however, is the question of how this political activity affects the other activities of congregational life. That is, how is the balance between internal activities—worship, education, fellowship—and outreach maintained in congregations that turn large portions of their organizational energy toward political engagement? At least some 1960s social activists think that the churches eventually "ran empty," as the moral energy for reform was spent. Similarly, some conservative activists have begun to question the wisdom of spending so much time on politics (Thomas and Dobson 1999).

The Public Work of Building Religious Communities

Maintaining that balance between internal maintenance and external engagement is no mean feat, especially given the challenge of building any voluntary community among today's diverse, scattered, and choice-driven members (Wuthnow 1998). Congregations retain significant degrees of racial and class homogeneity that only sometimes help to bridge social barriers (Wuthnow 2003). But even people who look alike often have lives that are increasingly disparate (Eiesland 2000). I have argued that part of the bridge-building civic function of congregations is in the way they teach people to work and worship together across lines of gender and generation, education and neighborhood, and sometimes also race and class (Ammerman 2005b). The very construction of a congregation requires civic skills of deliberation and bridge building. Any thriving congregation is constructed of complicated layers of connection. As Warner argues, congregations are "functionally diffuse" (Warner 1994). They do many things for the people who join them and the people with whom they are connected. They are spaces full of affective bonds, ideological commitments, instrumental necessities, and more. Those multiple layers have to be forged into a workable balance that may or may not include connections with people and organizations beyond the group itself.

Clearly not every congregation succeeds. Some are moribund. Some are so thinly constructed as to be irrelevant. Some worry so much about maintaining a warm and comforting fellowship that they shun any person or issue that might roil the waters. And as communities and demographics change, some are so consumed by their own internal conflict that they may drain energy out of the community rather than add any sort of civic or social capital. Indeed, both how congregations deal with conflict and how they engage larger civic and political issues are related to the basic cultural rules that shape their work (Becker 1997). Those that try to be most like extended families are most likely to avoid open debate and may not provide the range of civic practices and encouragement toward public engagement to be found in congregations that expect deliberation, debate, and even disagreement.

The Challenges of Diversity

Both within and between, congregations are by no means a monolithic phenomenon. They are as wildly varied as the American population itself. Each local community of faith reflects both the particular theological imperatives of its tradition and the cultural expectations of operating in America's voluntarist religious environment. As we have seen, some intend to equip their members for engagement in affairs of common life, while others do so more indirectly, and still others absorb the associational energy of their members in tight-knit fellowship.

What should also be clear is that these diverse faith communities will bring people together around diverse public causes. There is ample legal and cultural space for public engagement, whenever religious groups choose to do so; and they often have. Religious ideas have often mobilized public action in

U.S. history, and we can expect to continue to hear many different religious voices in U.S. public life. Sometimes those voices will articulate ideas in a manner broadly accessible to a diverse religious and secular public—in the "rational" and universalist terms usually equated with public communication (Habermas 1984). Sometimes, however, they will use other modes of discourse that may or may not be readily comprehensible to outsiders. They may introduce symbols and images that seem strange or even absurd. Indeed, sometimes they will be intentionally inflammatory. As we debate public goods, we will hear many moral voices, both religious and secular. Our constitutional system denies any of them the ability to impose their will on us. Our voluntarist denominational system encourages them to recognize their own partiality, but some will still speak as if their own truth should be accepted by everyone.

The differences among us will remain, and we have to be concerned about the effects on the larger polity of fostering separate particularistic communities where diverse issues and distinctive styles of engagement may be nurtured. My own inclination is to agree with those who argue that these separate, protected, religious spaces are in fact civically useful. As Warner argues, "Subcultural religious reproduction does not require antagonism towards one's neighbor. . . . In the United States, religious difference is the most legitimate cultural difference" (Warner 1999, 236). Local congregations that sustain and express those religious differences are essential to making the system work. Demerath agrees that congregations are a clue to the relative lack of religious violence in the United States. "In settings where a communal or congregational grouping is lacking, the faithful may be especially vulnerable to aberrant movements that offer an equivalent to the congregational experience while pursuing more secular and political agendas" (Demerath 2001, 218).

So I come again to the explicitly religious work of building robust religious traditions through the work of thousands of local congregations. We know that those congregations spend most of their energy on worship, religious education, and building a place where increasingly diverse groups find at least a temporary home. This basic congregational work requires constant voluntary investment if any local community of faith is to thrive. And, I am suggesting, there is good reason to suspect that it is work not wasted. Understanding how and whether that is the case remains an unfinished task. Under what circumstances does congregational life provide everyday skills for being together and working together with diverse others? And what range of strategies do congregations offer their members for understanding the relationship between their own traditions and the many others that surround them? Wuthnow's research on the challenges of diversity suggests that our range of strategies for engagement are still rather anemic, even if we are committed to the theoretical values of pluralism (Wuthnow 2005).

The American religious experiment continues as a wider and wider array of the world's religions try their hand at engendering voluntary religious commitment that is both rooted and tolerant. Local congregations form the base from which religious work is organized and a primary site where deeply held distinctions have been nurtured. If that were the whole story, we might have reason to be very worried. But for most, there are also well-established habits of partnership that create at least nascent networks out into a broader community. There are also habits of internal congregational life—organizing, debating, learning to get along with diverse others—that help to constitute the conversational habits on which civic life depends. We know enough to know that American congregations are critical sites on the civic landscape. They are sites that deserve continued attention as we attempt to understand how civic life works.

Notes

1. It should be noted that this presumed conflict also rests on the mistaken assumption that "civic life" requires exclusively "rational" deliberation conducted in universally available public spaces. For a critique of this assumption, see Fraser (1990). Religion as "nonrational" and not modern is an idea often attributed to Max Weber (1947), although his arguments were far more subtle than that. A more recent exponent is Jürgen Habermas (1976). The offhanded equation of religion with the pursuit of truth, and thus its potential incivility, is also present in work by Alexander (1992) and Friedland and Alford (1991). Thiemann (1996) offers an eloquent philosophical alternative to this view.

2. Writing against this view are Stephen Carter (1993) and Richard Neuhaus (1984).

3. All statistics calculated by the author from the General Social Survey (NORC 2005).

4. Among those who have explored the tension between the internal bonds of religious groups and their ability to "bridge" into the civic arena are Wuthnow (1999, 2003), Putnam (2000), and Chaves (2004).

5. I would not agree, however, with Stark that monotheism itself leads to incivility (Stark 2001).

6. The "evangelistic" mission orientation described by Roozen, McKinney, and Carroll (1984) exemplifies the connection between otherworldly focus and absence of social activism in this world.

7. A recent poll for *Religion and Ethics Newsweekly* suggests that when parents talk about the values they want to pass on to their children, first on their list are honesty and responsibility (Greenberg Quinlan Rosner Research 2005). It is likely that our respondents had similar values in mind when they affirmed the importance of living Christian values.

8. These findings are reported in full in Ammerman (2005b). The importance of church attendance for community participation and volunteering is also documented by Wuthnow (1999). His findings show that "regular" attenders differ from infrequent attenders in joining community organizations, volunteering for some types of service activities, and voting. Robin Gill (1999) works from both theories of Christian ethics and British poll data to show how church participation affects morality. See also Hodgkinson et al. (1990). Park and Smith (2000) also find that participation in "church activities" (presumably beyond worship) is a strong and consistent predictor of volunteering in nonchurch organizations. Michael Stoll (2001) shows that church attendance is a key link in channeling poor blacks into other voluntary organizations. John Wilson and Thomas Janoski (1995) present a more complicated picture, arguing that church activism has positive effects on nonchurch volunteering only for liberals and Catholics.

9. The involvement of congregations in community service is documented in Ammerman (2005a). See also Chaves (1999, 2004), Cnaan et al. (2002), and Hodgkinson and Weitzman (1993).

Works Cited

Aho, James A. 1990. *The Politics of Righteousness: Idaho Christian Patriotism*. Seattle: University of Washington Press.

Alexander, Jeffrey. 1992. "Citizen and Enemy as Symbolic Classification: On the Polarizing Discourse of Civil Society." In *Cultivating Differences: Symbolic Boundaries and the Making of Inequality*, M. Lamont and M. Fournier, eds., 289–308. Chicago: University of Chicago Press.

Ammerman, Nancy T. 1997. "Golden Rule Christianity: Lived Religion in the American Mainstream." In *Lived Religion in America: Toward a History of Practice*, D. Hall, ed., 196–216. Princeton, NJ: Princeton University Press.

———. 2002. "Grieving Together: September 11 as a Measure of Social Capital in the U.S." In *September 11: Religious Perspectives on the Causes and Consequences*, I. Abu Rabi, ed., 53–73. London: Oneworld Publications.

———. 2005a. *Pillars of Faith: American Congregations and Their Partners*. Berkeley: University of California Press.

―――. 2005b. "Religious Narratives, Community Service, and Everyday Public Life." In *Taking Faith Seriously: Valuing and Evaluating Religion in American Democracy*, M. J. Bane, B. Coffin, and R. Higgins, eds., 146–74. Cambridge, MA: Harvard University Press.

Bane, Mary Jo. 2005. "The Catholic Puzzle: Parishes and Civic Lives." In *Taking Faith Seriously: Valuing and Evaluating Religion in American Democracy*, M. J. Bane, B. Coffin, and R. Higgins, eds., 63–93. Cambridge, MA: Harvard University Press.

Becker, Penny Edgell. 1997. "What Is Right? What Is Caring? Moral Logics in Local Religious Life." In *Contemporary American Religion*, P. E. Becker and N. L. Eiesland, eds., 121–46. Beverly Hills, CA: Alta Mira.

Becker, Penny Edgell, and Pawan H. Dhingra. 2001. "Religious Involvement and Volunteering: Implications for Civil Society." *Sociology of Religion* 62, no. 3:315–35.

Bellah, Robert N. 1963. "Civil Religion in America." In *Beyond Belief*. Boston: Beacon.

Beyerlein, Kraig, and Mark Chaves. 2003. "The Political Activities of Religious Congregations in the United States." *Journal for the Scientific Study of Religion* 42, no. 2:229–46.

Butler, Jon. 1990. *Awash in a Sea of Faith*. Cambridge, MA: Harvard University Press.

Carter, Stephen L. 1993. *The Culture of Disbelief*. New York: Basic Books.

Casanova, Jose. 1994. *Public Religions in the Modern World*. Chicago: University of Chicago Press.

Chaves, Mark. 1999. "Congregations' Social Service Activities." Washington, DC: The Urban Institute.

―――. 2004. *Congregations in America*. Cambridge, MA: Harvard University Press.

Cnaan, Ram A. 1999. *The Newer Deal: Social Work and Religion in Partnership*. New York: Columbia University Press.

Cnaan, Ram A., Stephanie C. Boddie, Femida Handy, Gaynor I. Yancey, and Richard Schneider. 2002. *The Invisible Caring Hand: American Congregations and the Provision of Welfare*. New York: New York University Press.

Davis, Stephen P., Juan R. Martinez, and R. Stephen Warner. 2007. "The Role of the Catholic Church in the Chicago Immigrant Mobilization." Paper presented at Marching for Change: Chicago in the National Immigrant Movement, March 1, at the University of Illinois Chicago.

Demerath, N. J. 2001. *Crossing the Gods: World Religions and Worldly Politics*. New Brunswick, NJ: Rutgers University Press.

Edgell, Penny, Joseph Gerteis, and Douglas Hartmann. 2006. "Atheists as 'Other': Moral Boundaries and Cultural Membership in American Society." *American Sociological Review* 71, no. 2:211–34.

Eiesland, Nancy. 2000. *A Particular Place: Urban Restructuring and Religious Ecology*. New Brunswick, NJ: Rutgers University Press.

Fish, Stanley. 2007. "Religion Without Truth." *New York Times*, March 31, 2007. http://select.nytimes.com/gst/abstract.html?res=F20F10F83A540C728FDDAA0894DF 404482 (accessed April 9, 2007).

Fraser, Nancy. 1990. "Rethinking the Public Sphere: A Contribution to the Critique of Actually Existing Democracy." *Social Text* 25, no. 26:56–80.

Friedland, Roger, and Robert R. Alford. 1991. "Bringing Society Back In: Symbols, Practices, and Institutional Contradictions." In *The New Institutionalism in Organizational Analysis*, W. Powell and P. DiMaggio, eds., 232–63. Chicago: University of Chicago Press.

Gill, Robin. 1999. *Churchgoing and Christian Ethics*. Cambridge: Cambridge University Press.

Greeley, Andrew M. 1972. *The Denominational Society*. Glenview, IL: Scott-Foresman.

Greenberg Quinlan Rosner Research. 2005. "Faith and Family in America." *Religion & Ethics Newsweekly*, October 19, 2005. http://www.pbs.org/wnet/religio nandethics/week908/ReligionAndFamily_Summary.pdf (accessed November 28, 2005).

Habermas, Jürgen. 1976. *Communication and the Evolution of Society*. Boston: Beacon.

———. 1984. *The Theory of Communicative Action*. Boston: Beacon Press.

Hadaway, C. Kirk, Penny Long Marler, and Mark Chaves. 1993. "What the Polls Don't Show: A Closer Look at U.S. Church Attendance." *American Sociological Review* 58, no. 6:741–52.

Handy, Robert T. 1972. *Religion in the American Experience: The Pluralistic Style*. New York: Harper & Row.

Hatch, Nathan G. 1989. *The Democratization of American Christianity*. New Haven, CT: Yale University Press.

Hodgkinson, Virginia A., and Murray S. Weitzman. 1993. "From Belief to Commitment: The Community Service Activities and Finances of Religious Congregations in the United States: 1993 Edition." Washington, DC: Independent Sector.

Hodgkinson, Virginia A., Murray S. Weitzman, and Arthur D. Kirsch. 1990. "From Commitment to Action: How Religious Involvement Affects Giving and Volunteering." In *Faith and Philanthropy in America: Exploring the Role of Religion in America's Voluntary Sector*, R. Wuthnow and V. A. Hodgkinson, eds., 93–114. San Francisco: Jossey-Bass.

Hout, Michael, and Claude Fischer. 2002. "Why More Americans Have No Religious Preference: Politics and Generations." *American Sociological Review* 67: 165–90.

Lichterman, Paul. 2005. *Elusive Togetherness: Church Groups Trying to Bridge America's Divisions*. Princeton, NJ: Princeton University Press.

————. 2006. "A Place on the Map: Communicating Religious Presence in Civic Life." In *Everyday Religion: Observing Modern Religious Lives*, N. T. Ammerman, ed., 137–51. New York: Oxford University Press.

Mead, Sidney E. 1963. *The Lively Experiment*. New York: Harper & Row.

Milofsky, Carl, and Albert Hunter. 1995. "Where Nonprofits Come From: A Theory of Organizational Emergence." Paper presented at Southern Sociological Society, April, Atlanta, Georgia.

Moon, Dawne. 2004. *God, Sex, and Politics: Homosexuality and Everyday Theologies*. Chicago: University of Chicago Press.

Munson, Ziad. 2006. "When a Funeral Isn't Just a Funeral: The Layered Meaning of Everyday Action." In *Everyday Religion: Observing Modern Religious Lives*, N. T. Ammerman, ed., 121–35. New York: Oxford University Press.

Musick, Marc A., John Wilson, and William B. Bynum Jr. 2000. "Race and Formal Volunteering: The Differential Effects of Class and Religion." *Social Forces* 78, no. 4:1539–71.

Neuhaus, Richard J. 1984. *The Naked Public Square*. Grand Rapids, MI: Eerdmans.

NORC (National Opinion Research Center). 2005. *GSSDIRS General Social Survey: 1972–2000 Cumulative Codebook*. National Opinion Research Center at the University of Chicago 2001. http://webapp.icpsr.umich.edu/GSS/ (accessed July 4, 2005).

Orr, John B., Donald E. Miller, Wade Clark Roof, and J. Gordon Melton. 1994. *Politics of the Spirit: Religion and Multiethnicity in Los Angeles*. Los Angeles: University of Southern California.

Park, Jerry Z., and Christian Smith. 2000. "'To Whom Much Has Been Given . . .': Religious Capital and Community Voluntarism among Church-Going Protestants." *Journal for the Scientific Study of Religion* 39, no. 3:272–86.

Paxton, Pamela. 2002. "Social Capital and Democracy: An Interdependent Relationship." *American Sociological Review* 67, no. 2:254–77.

Putnam, Robert D. 2000. *Bowling Alone: The Collapse and Revival of American Community*. New York: Simon & Schuster.

Roozen, David A., William McKinney, and Jackson W. Carroll. 1984. *Varieties of Religious Presence*. New York: Pilgrim Press.

Sherman, Amy. 2000. "Churches as Government Partners: Navigating 'Charitable Choice.'" *Christian Century* 117, no. 20:716–21.

Smidt, Corwin, ed. 2003. *Religion as Social Capital: Producing the Common Good*. Waco, TX: Baylor University Press.

Smith, Christian. 1998. *American Evangelicalism: Embattled and Thriving*. Chicago: University of Chicago Press.

————. 2000. *Christian America? What Evangelicals Really Want*. Berkeley: University of California Press.

Stark, Rodney. 2001. *One True God: Historical Consequences of Monotheism*. Princeton, NJ: Princeton University Press.

Stoll, Michael. 2001. "Race, Neighborhood Poverty, and Participation in Voluntary Associations." *Sociological Forum* 16, no. 3:529–57.

Thiemann, Ronald F. 1996. *Religion in Public Life: A Dilemma for Democracy*. Washington, DC: Georgetown University Press.

Thomas, Cal, and Ed Dobson. 1999. *Blinded by Might: Can the Religious Right Save America?* Grand Rapids, MI: Zondervan.

Verba, Sidney, Kay Lehman Schlozman, and Henry E. Brady. 1995. *Voice and Equality: Civic Voluntarism in American Politics*. Cambridge, MA: Harvard University Press.

Warner, R. Stephen. 1993. "Work in Progress Toward a New Paradigm for the Sociological Study of Religion in the United States." *American Journal of Sociology* 98, no. 5:1044–93.

———. 1994. "The Place of the Congregation in the Contemporary American Religious Configuration." In *American Congregations: New Perspectives in the Study of Congregations*, J. Wind and J. Lewis, eds., 54–99. Chicago: University of Chicago Press.

———. 1999. "Changes in the Civic Role of Religion." In *Diversity and Its Discontents: Cultural Conflict and Common Ground in Contemporary American Society*, N. J. Smelser and J. C. Alexander, eds., 229–43. Princeton, NJ: Princeton University Press.

Washington, George. [1796] 2007. "Farewell Address to the People of the United States." *Archiving Early America 1796*. http://www.earlyamerica.com/earlyamerica/milestones/farewell/text.html (accessed April 9, 2007).

Weber, Max. 1947. *The Theory of Social and Economic Organization*. A. M. Henderson and T. Parsons, trans. New York: Free Press.

Wilson, John, and Thomas Janoski. 1995. "The Contribution of Religion to Volunteer Work." *Sociology of Religion* 56, no. 2:137–52.

Wolfe, Alan. 2003. *The Transformation of American Religion*. New York: Free Press.

Wuthnow, Robert. 1998. *Loose Connections: Joining Together in America's Fragmented Communities*. Cambridge, MA: Harvard University Press.

———. 1999. "Mobilizing Civic Engagement: The Changing Impact of Religious Involvement." In *Civic Engagement in American Democracy*, T. Skocpol and M. P. Fiorina, eds., 331–63. Washington, DC: Brookings Institution Press.

———. 2002. "Beyond Quiet Influence? Possibilities for the Protestant Mainline." In *Quietly Influential: The Public Role of Mainline Protestantism*, R. Wuthnow and J. Evans, eds., 381–404. Berkeley: University of California Press.

———. 2003. "Overcoming Status Distinctions? Religious Involvement, Social Class, Race, and Ethnicity in Friendship Patterns." *Sociology of Religion* 64, no. 4:423–42.

————. 2005. *America and the Challenges of Religious Diversity*. Princeton, NJ: Princeton University Press.

Wuthnow, Robert, and John H. Evans, eds. 2002. *The Quiet Hand of God: Faith-Based Activism and the Public Role of Mainline Protestantism*. Berkeley: University of California Press.

4 Congregations' Significance to American Civic Life

Mark Chaves

THE ROLE OF RELIGION IN GENERAL, and congregations in particular, in modern societies is a complex and multifaceted subject. It is a subject of long-standing normative concern to religious leaders, but recent debates about declining social capital, trends in civic engagement, and the health of civil society have increased interest in this subject among social scientists and policymakers, especially in the United States, where religious organizations make up a sizable portion of civil society, however that is defined and however one counts.

In this chapter I explore the theme of religious congregations' significance to American civic life in two ways. By "religious congregations" I mean local places of worship—the churches, synagogues, and mosques that are so common in American communities. First, I will examine what congregations do, and I will start by focusing on their social service activities. This is an appropriate place to start because we recently have seen a movement to direct more public resources to religious organizations in support of their social service activities. The movement's most visible face has been the Bush presidential administration's "faith-based initiative." Though past its heyday, this movement lives on, now largely beneath the radar, as a set of loosely coordinated legislative, administrative, and cultural initiatives at all levels of government, held together by the common goal of directing more tax money to certain kinds of religious organizations in support of their social service work.

These efforts raise many issues and questions, some of which are not at all new. Congregations have been engaged in human service work for a very long time, they have received government support for their social service work for a very long time, and at least since the Social Gospel movement of the early twentieth century there have been those who call on congregations to do more to meet human needs. Recent efforts and debate associated with faith-based initiatives, however, have increased public interest in congregations' social service work, and this increased interest provides an opportunity to examine this work more closely than we otherwise might. I think this is worth doing, not least because there is much misunderstanding afoot about congregations' social service work and, more generally, about what congregations do, how they do and do not contribute to American society, and how to think about their significance to American public life. So focusing on congregations' social service activities provides a useful launching point for a more general discussion of what congregations do, and their place in American civic life.

As we will see, for most congregations social service work is not central to their collective life. Therefore I will step back from some issues raised directly by current debates about congregation-based social services in order to say in a positive way what congregations do when they are not doing social services, which is most of the time. Much of this first part of the chapter will draw on the National Congregations Study, a 1998 survey of a nationally representative sample of 1,236 congregations from across the religious spectrum. These data are very informative about the kinds of things congregations do, and it is relatively easy to describe what the average or typical congregation does. It is much more difficult, however, to assess the significance to American civic life of what congregations do. This is the issue I will wrestle with in the second part of the chapter by examining congregations' share of activity in various secular arenas. I will shift attention, in other words, from what kinds of activities are significant *for congregations* to congregations' significance for different arenas of activity.

Congregations' Social Service Activities

Two Myths

To give my description of congregations' social service activities a bit of an edge, I will identify two common assumptions about congregations and social services and then argue that neither assumption is borne out by the evidence. These assumptions turn out to be myths. There are many more than two myths on this subject circulating in conventional wisdom, but here I will limit attention to just two of the most important myths. The first and probably most important myth is that the typical congregation is intensively involved in social service activities. The reality is that virtually all congregations do something that might be called social service, but much of this activity is very small-scale and informal and focused on short-term, emergency needs for food, clothing, and shelter. Fifty-seven percent of congregations reported some sort of social service activity in the National Congregations Study; three-quarters of churchgoers are in these congregations. This understates the extent to which congregations provide very informal and small-scale kinds of assistance to needy people beyond their own membership, but I think it gives an accurate picture of the proportion of congregations doing more or less formal kinds of social service activities.

What kinds of programs are congregations typically involved in? Food programs, reported by one-third of congregations, are most common, followed by shelter programs, clothing programs, and, related to activities focused on housing and shelter, services to the homeless. Importantly, the percentages of involved congregations get very small when looking at more serious, intensive, long-term-need kinds of programs: Five percent are involved in health programs, 2 percent in substance abuse prevention programs, and 1 percent in employment-related programs. The basic picture is that the typical kind of congregation-based social service activity is focused on short-term, emergency needs. More intensive, personalistic, transforming kinds of social service are engaged in by only the rare congregation.

These numbers do not speak directly to the issue of how intensively congregations are involved in social services because there could be much variation in intensity behind these numbers. A food program could be anything from collecting canned goods at Thanksgiving to running a soup kitchen; housing could be anything from a Habitat for Humanity project, in which a small group of volunteers works on a house for several months, to building low-income housing. Here are several more direct measures of the intensity of congregational involvement in social services: Six percent of congregations have a staff person working at least quarter time on social services. The median congregation doing social services mentions just two programs. The median amount of money those congregations spend on social services is $1,200, which is 2–3 percent of the median budget. And the median congregation doing social services reports only ten volunteers involved in these activities.

There are, of course, some congregations that are deeply engaged in social services, and they are important. I don't mean to trivialize the absolute amount of social service activity that occurs in congregations. We should keep in mind that even if only 1 percent of congregations is deeply involved in social services, 1 percent of 300,000 congregations in the United States is still 3,000 congregations doing significant work of this sort. But the key point here is that those congregations are the exception, not the rule. The vast majority of congregations are involved in social services in only a peripheral and superficial way.

A second myth is that congregation-based social services represent an alternative to the world of secular and government-funded social services. The assumption here is that there are large amounts of congregation-based social services that are entirely bottom-up and voluntary in the sense of being initiated and fully supported by the voluntary action and donations of people in the congregation, and that this world of congregation-based services offers an alternative—some think a superior alternative—to the world of secular and government-funded social services. The truth is that when congregations are doing more than superficial social services, their activity is almost always done in collaboration with secular nonprofits and with government, and that activity often, maybe even almost always, is *dependent* on those collaborations and the support that comes from government and secular social service agencies.

Let us consider, for example, programs that feed the hungry. The soup kitchen is one of the most common forms of congregational involvement in social services. On the surface, it appears to be the quintessential case of a social service provided largely by religious organizations operating on their own, supported only by their own material and volunteer resources. But this surface appearance is misleading. A study of congregation-based feeding programs in Tucson, Arizona, for example, conducted by Rebecca Sager and her colleagues (2001), revealed that virtually all of these programs used food that came from the local food bank, a secular nonprofit organization, and virtually all relied on grants from the city to pay someone to cook the food and someone else to deliver it to the congregations each evening, where volunteers then distributed it to hungry people. The congregations are an important part of this system—they provide volunteers to serve the food and space in which people can eat it—but they would not be able to do this work absent a three-way collaboration among the congregations, a secular nonprofit organization, and the city. It is mistaken to imagine that all this laudable activity is occurring in a pristine religious voluntary sector unsullied by government or secular organizations. So congregations are not, in general, intensively involved in social services, and when they do conduct serious social services they do so in a way that often is dependent on substantial external support and collaborations.

To add a positive note, there is, in fact, a distinctive congregational approach to social services. It just is not the approach assumed in much conventional wisdom about congregations. When congregations do more than collect canned goods at Thanksgiving, the characteristic congregational approach to social service—and something they are very good at—is to mobilize small groups of volunteers to do well-defined, bounded tasks on a periodic basis: For example, five people cook dinner once a week at the homeless shelter, ten people spend six Saturdays fixing or building a house or apartment, or the youth group spends two summer weeks painting a school. If we were serious about involving congregations more deeply and intensively in social service work, we would look for ways to use this particular resource. This is the genius of Habitat for Humanity, and it is why congregations and congregation-based groups are so prevalent in the world of homeless shelters and feeding programs for the hungry. These programs know how to use this particular kind of resource that congregations are very good, perhaps uniquely good, at providing.

What Do Congregations Do?

If congregations do not do much social service activity, what *do* they do? Congregations gather people for worship and religious education. This is painfully obvious, and I am always somewhat embarrassed to feel the need to make this point, but one of the odd features of our current cultural moment is that it seems necessary to point out that although most congregations do some social services, and although a very small percentage of congregations do a lot of social services, congregations are not, fundamentally and essentially, social service providers.

Yet there is more to say that is not quite so obvious. Worship and religious education are congregations' core activities, but the pursuit of these core activities also generates by-products, so speak, and it is reasonable to ask what the most significant by-product is. In these days of faith-based initiatives we focus on social services as a significant by-product of congregations' core activities. Since the 1980s rise of the religious right we also have focused on politics as a by-product of congregational activity. But the truth is that neither politics nor social services are significant activities for the vast majority of congregations. Something else is, though, and that's art.

No one doubts the historical connection between religion and art, but today we mainly think of art and religion as two largely distinct, perhaps even opposed, arenas. This opposition seems plausible if we limit our attention to *high* art. But if we define artistic practice more broadly as the making, seeing, or listening to music, dance, drama, and objects for display, whatever the venue, the quality of the product, or whether it is pursued as an end in itself, then the intimate connection between art and religion—especially religion as it is practiced in congregations—becomes clear, mainly, of course, because worship services are constructed in part out of artistic elements like music, drama, poetry, and dance.

The case is clearest with music, though the point is not limited to music. Fifty-seven percent of congregations reported social services in the last year, and 42 percent reported some sort of political activity, but virtually all expose people to live music every single week. The worship service experienced by the average attender in the United States has twenty minutes of music and lasts for seventy minutes, which means more than one-quarter of worship is music. And almost 80 percent of congregations had some sort of *non*musical arts activity in the last year, meaning mainly drama or dance. A lot of this arts-related activity happens in worship, but a substantial amount happens outside of worship as well: Thirty-eight percent of congregations had a group put on a musical or theatrical performance; 43 percent had a group that attended a live performance elsewhere.

More congregations engage in the arts than in social services or politics, but it's not just that more congregations engage in arts. Their artistic activities also involve more people than their social service or political activities. Seventy people attend the average worship service; in congregations with choirs, twenty people are in the average choir. Compare that to the number involved in other ancillary activities: In congregations with social service programs, the median number of people involved with these programs as volunteers is ten. On average, only fifteen people in a congregation regularly meet in small groups for any purpose other than worship, religious education, or internal administration.

Artistic activity also takes up more staff time than either social services or politics. Jackson Carroll's recent (2006) national survey of clergy found that full-time clergy spend fifteen hours per week in worship or preparing for worship; they spend only one to two hours weekly working with community or civic groups. Recall that only 6 percent of congregations have a staff person devoting at least quarter time to social service work; the National Congregations Study did not ask how many congregations employ organists or music directors, but it seems safe to assume that many more than 6 percent do.

No one will be surprised at the centrality of worship and religious education to congregational life. The prevalence of artistic activities, relative to politics or social services, is more surprising. Although the social gospel enthusiasts among us might wish it were otherwise, if we ask what congregations do beyond their core activities of worship and religious education, the answer is that they facilitate art, and perhaps, on occasion, even beauty, more commonly and more intensively than they dispense charity or pursue justice.

Congregations' Share of Public Arenas

I have focused so far on assessing the significance of various kinds of activities *to congregations*. Because of the National Congregations Study and other recent studies of congregations, we now know quite a lot about what congregations do and the relative significance of civic volunteering and political and artistic activities *for them*. On the flip side, assessing congregations' larger public significance requires asking what proportion of the action in public arenas is based in congregations rather than what proportion of congregational life is taken up by various kinds of activities. We need to assess not just the relative importance of art, social service, and politics to congregations; we also need to assess the relative importance of congregations to the larger worlds of art, social service, and politics. In each of these arenas we would like to assess the extent to which congregations are significant actors or venues or facilitators of action. This is very difficult to assess, and I know of no data that can definitively nail this down. Surveys of congregations alone will not do the trick. But I draw on a variety of data sources to cobble what I think is a reasonably strong circumstantial case that not only is artistic activity more important to congregations than social services or politics, but congregations are more important to the artistic arena than they are to either the political or the social services arena.[1]

Congregations' Share of Live Arts

Available evidence suggests that a substantial proportion of all live arts activity occurs in congregations. We can see this by drawing on surveys of arts participation in order to compare the percentage of people who experience live music, dance, and drama in congregations with the percentage who experience it anywhere. The case is strongest with music. In 1998, two-thirds of American adults claimed to have attended a religious service within the past twelve months. More than 95 percent of those attendees participated in a service with singing by the congregation, more than 90 percent heard a musical instrument being played, and more than 70 percent heard singing by a choir. Half of religious service attendees heard a soloist. This means that more than 60 percent of Americans participated in, or at least heard, group singing in a congregation in the past year, 60 percent heard an instrument being played in a congregation, and one-third heard a soloist in a congregation.

In that same year, by contrast, 17 percent of American adults claimed to have attended a classical music concert and 39 percent claimed to have attended a pop music concert in the past twelve months. Twenty-five percent saw a musical play, 12 percent saw a jazz performance, and 5 percent saw live opera. Especially if we consider the frequency with which people attend religious services compared with these other events at which live music is heard, it becomes clear that worship services constitute the vast majority of the live musical events experienced by people in American society. Congregations' worship services, where 60 percent of the population hears live music in a given year, are the single most common type of event at which live music is heard in American society. It probably is not the case that the majority of live dance and drama experienced by Americans is experienced in congregations, but even when it comes to live dance and drama, a nontrivial amount is experienced in congregations.

Comparing Congregations' Share of Arts with Their Share of Social Services and Politics

If Americans experience a substantial proportion of live art in congregations, how does this compare with the proportion of all social services and politics occurring in and through congregations? It is very difficult to find valid ways and relevant data to compare congregations' share of live arts activity with their share of political and social service activity. Given the current state of knowledge, the claim that congregations' share of all artistic activity in the society is greater than their share of all social service and political activity remains conjecture rather than established fact. Still, several kinds of indirect evidence suggest that such a conjecture is not entirely fanciful. Here are four points of comparison.

First, regarding social services, Robert Wuthnow and his colleagues (2003) surveyed individuals in the fifteen inner-city census tracts with the lowest median household incomes in the Lehigh Valley. The research team first identified all the major social service providers in the area, none of which were congregations. Respondents were then asked whether they had contacted each of these social service agencies for assistance and also whether they had contacted a congregation for assistance. Forty percent of the respondents who contacted any organization contacted a secular nonprofit organization, 36 percent the public welfare department, 28 percent a religious social service organization that was not a congregation, and only 22 percent a congregation.

There are specific domains within the larger social services arena—feeding the hungry, for example—in which congregations' share is larger than their share of the arena as a whole. It seems unlikely, however, that there is a sub-arena as important to the social services world as music is to the arts world, and in which congregations' share approaches their share of all live music performance in the society. Moreover, although congregations connect to both the social services and the cultural realms sometimes as congregations and sometimes as mere physical locations for activities that do not involve the congregations' people, the relative importance of these two modes of connecting is different in social services than it is in the arts. *Congregations* seem more important in the social services arena as providers of physical space than as providers, qua congregations, of social services. The opposite is true for the arts. There, mainly but not only because of the intimate connection between worship and the arts, congregations seem more significant as providers of arts experiences qua congregations than as mere venues for performances. It seems reasonable to weigh congregational participation in an activity more heavily when the congregation is involved as a congregation than when it is involved only by virtue of its physical space. All things considered, even though congregations are noticeably present in some social service sub-arenas, it is difficult to see how their share of all the social service activity occurring in American society could approach their share of all live artistic activity in the society.

A second point of comparison uses data gathered by Sidney Verba and his colleagues to contrast congregations' relative importance in the artistic arena with their relative importance in the political arena (Verba et al. 1995). They found that more individuals are asked to be politically active in their congregations than in their workplaces or in other nonpolitical organizations, but significantly fewer are asked to be politically active in congregations than in explicitly political organizations. Thirty-two percent of Americans are asked to vote or to take other political action (sign a petition, write a letter, or get in touch with a public official) through their association with a political organization, compared with 23 percent who are asked to do these things through congregations, 13 percent who are asked to do these things in the workplace, and 6 percent who are asked to do these things through other nonpolitical organizations. From this perspective, congregations are visible players in the political arena—more visible, perhaps, than in the social services arena—but 40 percent more people receive political cues from specifically political associations than from congregations. Recall, by contrast, that congregations are the single most important sites for the consumption of live music.

A third comparison also involves politics. Here, we can draw again on the data gathered by Sidney Verba and his colleagues (1995), but this time to compare congregations' significance as sites for practicing civic skills relative to their significance as sites for practicing artistic skills. When it comes to venues for exercising the kinds of civic skills that lead to more effective political participation, the workplace is much more significant than either congregations or other nonpolitical organizations. More than twice as many people attend meetings where decisions are made in their workplaces as in their congregations (46 percent versus 21 percent), more than twice as many plan such meetings in workplaces as in congregations (23 percent versus 11 percent), more than twice as many make a speech or presentation in workplaces as in congregations (26 percent versus 12 percent), and more than four times as many write a letter in the workplace as in a congregation (39 percent versus 8 percent).

Compare these indications of the relative importance of congregations in providing opportunities to exercise civic skills with the relative importance of congregations in providing opportunities to exercise at least one sort of artistic skill. Virtually all congregations sing together, which means that two-thirds of all Americans have the opportunity to sing in congregations at least once a year. This is compared with 11 percent of individuals who say they have performed music, dance, or theater; 24 percent who play a musical instrument; 8 percent who sing music from musical plays; and 2 percent who sing opera music. At least as far as singing is concerned, congregations provide a far larger share of the opportunities for exercising this artistic skill than they provide for exercising the civic skills studied by Verba and his colleagues.

People do not just passively consume art in congregations. They do not just listen to music, for example. They sing and play music as well, and it seems that a bigger share of artistic skills than of civic skills is exercised in congregations.

A fourth and final comparison comes from the 2003 American Time Use Survey (Bureau of Labor Statistics 2005). This study enables us to assess congregations' significance to art and social service arenas as sites for volunteer activity. Respondents to this survey recounted everything they did over the course of a day, and respondents were asked where they did the activities they reported. When we examine the locational patterns for various kinds of volunteering, we find that 24 percent of all volunteering to prepare or serve food occurred in a place of worship, as did 13 percent of all volunteering connected to collecting or delivering clothes or other goods and 13 percent of "direct care" (for example, reading to blind people) volunteering. At the same time, by contrast, *two-thirds* of the volunteering in connection with cultural events occurred in places of worship. This includes acting or dancing in a performance, performing music, emceeing a charity function, or ushering for a performance. These data are limited and inexact in various ways, but still they suggest that congregations account for a larger share of cultural and artistic volunteering than they do of social service volunteering.

Because data limitations preclude establishing firmly congregations' numerical shares of all activity in the artistic, social service, and political arenas, it is not clear whether one should say that congregations' share of arts activity is "a lot" while their share of political or social service activity is "a little," or to say that their share of politics and social services is "a lot" but their share of arts activity is "really a lot." Still, the available evidence, with all its limits, suggests that congregations' share of all live arts activity in American society is indeed more than their share of all political or social service activity. Congregations apparently account for a bigger share of all political activity in American society than they do of all social service activity, but they account for a bigger share of all activity in the cultural arena than in the social services or politics arenas. In this sense, congregations are a more significant organizational base for live arts than they are for social services or politics.

If we look for the public arena of American social life in which congregations are most a part we find it in the arts, not in social services or politics. Prominent voices in recent policy debates have emphasized a view of congregations as efficient nodes of civic virtue that can accomplish more compassionately with volunteers what governmental social service agencies accomplish less compassionately and less efficiently with tax money. This chapter provides an important corrective to conventional wisdom about the nature of congregations' contributions in these arenas.

Notes

A longer version of this chapter was first published in Antonius Liedhegener and Werner Kremp, eds., *Civil Society, Civic Engagement and Catholicism in the U.S.*, vol. 27 of Atlantische Texte (Trier: Wissenschaftlicher Verlag Trier, 2007), 31–43. Much of the material in this chapter is drawn from the book *Congregations in America* (Chaves 2004). Readers interested in more details or additional evidence supporting the arguments made in this chapter should consult the book itself.

1. Readers interested in more details and more supporting evidence for this claim can find them in Chaves (2004, chapter 7). Numbers mentioned below concerning Americans' participation in arts events are from either Marsden (1999, 2001) or National Endowment for the Arts (1998). Results in Wuthnow et al. (2003) are used for assessing congregations' share of social service activity, and results in Verba et al. (1995) are used for assessing congregations' share of political activity. Information about the relative importance of congregations as sites of various kinds of volunteering are from the 2003 American Time Use Survey, conducted and disseminated by the U.S. Bureau of Labor Statistics.

Works Cited

Bureau of Labor Statistics and United States Census Bureau. 2005. *American Time Use Survey User's Guide: 2003–2004.* http://www.bls.gov/tus/atususersguide.pdf.

Carroll, Jackson W. 2006. *God's Potters: Pastoral Leadership and the Shaping of Congregations.* Grand Rapids, MI: William B. Eerdmans Publishing Company.

Chaves, Mark. 2004. *Congregations in America.* Cambridge, MA: Harvard University Press.

Chaves, Mark, Helen M. Giesel, and William Tsitsos. 2002. "Religious Variations in Public Presence: Evidence from the National Congregations Study." In *The Quiet Hand of God: Faith-Based Activism and the Public Role of Mainline Protestantism*, Robert Wuthnow and John H. Evans, eds., 108–28. Berkeley: University of California Press.

Marsden, Peter V. 1999. "Religion, Cultural Participation, and Cultural Attitudes: Survey Data on the United States, 1998." Report to the Henry Luce Foundation, Department of Sociology, Harvard University.

————. 2001. "Religious Americans and the Arts in the 1990s." In *Crossroads: Art and Religion in American Life*, Alberta Arthurs and Glenn Wallach, eds., 71–102. New York: New Press.

National Endowment for the Arts. 1998. *1997 Survey of Public Participation in the Arts.* Research Division Report 39. Washington, DC: National Endowment for the Arts.

Sager, Rebecca, Laura S. Stephens, and Mary Nell Trautner. 2001. "Serving Up God? The Manifestations of Religion in Faith-Based Social Service Organizations." Paper presented at the annual meetings of the American Sociological Association, August, Anaheim, CA.

Verba, Sidney, Kay Lehman Schlozman, and Henry E. Brady. 1995. *Voice and Equality: Civic Voluntarism in American Politics.* Cambridge, MA: Harvard University Press.

Wuthnow, Robert, Conrad Hackett, and Becky Yang Hsu. 2003. "The Effectiveness and Trustworthiness of Faith-Based and Other Service Organizations: A Study of Recipients' Perceptions." Paper presented at The Role of Faith-Based Organizations in the Social Welfare System research forum cosponsored by Independent Sector and Roundtable on Religion and Social Welfare, March, Washington, DC.

5 Beyond Savior, Victim, and Sinner: Neighborhood Civic Life and "Absent Presence" in the Religious District

Omar M. McRoberts

THIS CHAPTER ELABORATES SOME IDEAS INITIALLY presented in my book *Streets of Glory* (2003), which examines religious congregations in a poor, predominantly African American neighborhood in Boston called Four Corners. The book is based on a four-year ethnographic study of the religious institutions and emerging community revitalization efforts in that neighborhood. Since the mid-1980s, this neighborhood had been known for its high violent crime rate, poverty, and economic underdevelopment. In that sense it is not unlike the kinds of neighborhoods that ordinarily appear in studies of urban poverty, the urban underclass, or the "ghetto." What struck me about this neighborhood when I first began visiting in 1995, however, was the number of congregations located there. After walking around the area for several days, I realized that there were about twenty-nine congregations, nearly all housed in commercial storefronts (colloquially we would call these "storefront churches"). Although many of the clergy I interviewed occasionally fantasized about having big, freestanding churches, most were quite satisfied with their little storefront communities, and in fact were suspicious of larger churches, which they felt had sacrificed much of the spiritual authenticity available to those who gathered humbly as "two or three in Jesus' name."[1] In other words, these churches typically were not cycling out of their rented storefront status into some other more powerful, more acceptable property class.[2] These sacred commercial spaces are fixtures, at least until rent fluctuations, due for example to economic development, push them out.

The density and diversity of congregations in Four Corners, plus the fact that most of these churches were in commercial spaces, led me to coin the term "religious district" to describe Four Corners. Of the twenty-nine churches in this religious district, twenty-four belonged to the Holiness-Pentecostal-Apostolic constellation of churches. Although the neighborhood was predominantly African American, nearly half of the congregations were composed of immigrants from the West Indies, Central America, and South America. Meanwhile, community development corporations, community health centers, and other secular entities, the likes of which were spearheading all sorts of revitalization efforts in nearby locales, were nearly absent in Four Corners.

In the months that followed, I learned that there was deep cynicism among neighborhood residents about the presence of so many churches. That cynicism was not based merely on the fact that many of the latter rented storefront spaces. The same residents wanted merchants, for example, to rent those spaces. Storefront churches were thought to send a message to prospective merchants and others that the overall class profile of the neighborhood was too low to sustain commerce. Congregations worshipping in traditional church structures were not thought to broadcast this kind of status message.[3] As such, rather than being understood as something necessary for the generation of civic life in the neighborhood, churches appeared as something transgressive. They were ubiquitous and yet out of place. They broke tacit societal norms about where and how people should worship. They emerged from the depression of the neighborhood and bluntly reminded people of that depression by occupying otherwise vacant commercial spaces. They were undeniably present in a physical sense, and yet they seemed absent in many of the ways that mattered for civic engagement in this neighborhood.

Meanwhile, social science scholarship continues to identify religious institutions as uniquely effective cultivators of civic skill and connectivity (Cnaan 2002; Warren 2001; Wood 2002; Ammerman 2002; Verba et al. 1995; Putnam 2000). What civic function might we expect religion to play in a neighborhood like Four Corners, where there are nearly thirty churches, about which residents tend to be deeply cynical? If a poor neighborhood hosts a religious district, is it not reasonable to expect that neighborhood to buzz with civic activity? In identifying the religious district phenomenon, *Streets of Glory* attempts to push us beyond, or perhaps beneath, the cliché about poor neighborhoods of color containing little other than storefront churches and liquor stores, so that we might understand where this dense, diverse religious presence comes from, and why such a presence matters in the cultivation of neighborhood civic capacity. In the process, the book also attempts to advance our understanding of civic engagement by specifying one of the most common, and least understood, ways that "the civic" comes to life in urban contexts—that is, through religious institutions. As the remainder of this chapter will explain, however, religious institutions do not necessarily, or even normally, nourish a *neighborhood* civic orientation. I begin with a theoretical reflection on the connection between urban life and religious civic forms, then proceed to an empirical consideration of the "religious district" of Four Corners.

Religious Civic Life as Integral to the Urban Process

Streets of Glory presents a general statement about the relationship between religious institutions and urban processes, the latter including all of the economic, demographic, and cultural forces that shape city life. By extension this statement pertains to the connection between *civic life* and urban processes. The idea is that particular urban religious forms have their roots as much in broader urban dynamics as anything else, and at the same time those religious forms help to shape those ongoing urban dynamics—it is not necessarily just one or the other. In making this statement, the book is meant to overcome two tendencies in scholarship and policy. One tendency is to take the church mainly as a source of moral order and concerned social action, which religious people impose on the city for its own sake. Here, in other words, the church is the model civic institution. The other tendency is to view religious forms as mere reactions to, or even epiphenomena of, the urban process, incapable of proactive, creative agency amidst the maelstrom of city life. Both notions implicitly accept the idea that church and city are somehow profoundly separate.

I trace these tendencies to an incomplete adoption of ideas formulated in early twentieth-century sociology in the United States. During this period, sociologists such as Robert Park, Charles Cooley, and William Thomas borrowed insights from pragmatist philosophy to resolve the chicken-egg ontological tension between individual and society (Levine 1995). They proposed that the individual self is both a cause and a consequence of the social, so the two were not really separate in reality. The city, as a unique manifestation of the economic function of society, is then compared to an unconscious natural ecology, which both produces sentient individual selves and responds to the conscious actions of those urban selves. This is not unlike the traditional pastoral narrative, where the human being emerges from the earth, develops agricultural capacities, and begins to mold the very earth from which he or she emerged. Individuals continually adapt and react, both psychologically and materially, to the chaotic flux of the urban ecology; but at the same time these individuals are capable, through the process of collective civic engagement, of inventing moral orders to regulate and direct the urban flux, thereby mediating its effects on human lives. The neighborhood block club, mutual aid society, the church, synagogue, mosque, temple, and even the pool hall are civic forms conjured by sets of individuals to buffer them from the city's wild indifference.

The sociologies of urban religion that grew out of this tradition have tended to view the church either as the product of the city or as a generator of moral order for the city—but the notion of the church as both product and producer of the city has been neglected for the most part. The local church, which so much scholarship presents as a key feature of the American civic landscape, is viewed, on the one hand, as an epiphenomenon, a purely adaptive institution. Religious ecologists who emerged around the middle of the twentieth century were concerned with how churches variously responded to the swirling chaos of the city, and especially the unpredictable but inevitable and ultimately "natural" neighborhood demographic shifts that took place (Douglass 1927; Kincheloe 1964). Here the church was always the victim of the mysterious urban process, much as humans are victims of earthquakes and typhoons. The concern of these scholars was how churches could survive the storm, not how they might have contributed to the urban processes that buffeted them around. The storm swept up again in the 1960s and 1970s, and this time white churches in particular were trying to make sense of white flight from urban cores, which left them isolated in overwhelmingly black and poor inner cities. Scholarship followed, wondering how the churches would respond to the storm, not how the churches might be implicated in the storm as agents.

On the other hand the church is cast as the natural savior of the city given its inherently benevolent and moral mission. This perspective is problematic because it compares churches to an idealized moral order instead of taking churches seriously for the moral orders they believe they are upholding. When a church fails to offer the expected salvific urban moral order, the church may be depicted as a tragic failure at best, and at worst a parasite. At the time of this writing we are witnessing a switch to the "church as savior" mode, featuring, among other things, a social policy movement that calls on churches to heal and save the inner city from itself, much as social gospel and moral reform ministries tried to do in divergent ways at the turn of the twentieth century, during the heaviest periods of urbanization.[4] Recent scholarship reproduces this "savior" mode, as scholars ask not how religious institutions are constituted by broader urban processes, but whether churches can reduce recidivism rates, provide social services, prevent and interrupt youth delinquency, and revitalize poor neighborhoods. The implication is that religious institutions are sufficiently *distinct* from the social milieus in which these problems emerge, as to be ready-made panacea (Bennett et al., 1996).

It goes without saying that the idea of a clear separation between church and urban environment reflects the view of many religious people themselves. In the religious imagination, the city—whether cast as an unconscious, amoral confluence of natural forces; a hellish workshop where the Devil engineers individual moral failure; or a vast chessboard dominated by powerful capitalists, bureaucrats, and other sinners—often is understood as the antithesis of the church world, just as nature and humanity, body and mind, indeed body and soul, are radically distinguished in certain theological and philosophical schools. I encountered this view a great deal in churches, and later I will discuss a certain kind of urban religiosity that radically distinguishes the street from the church in a way that gives meaning to religious practice. Yet, at least from a sociological standpoint, we are not bound to take this as the total picture. The idea of a radically distinct church world, which can only act salvifically or react defensively, rests upon moral assumptions that should be the subject, not the underlying premise, of study.

Accounts assuming at the outset that religious forms are mere symptoms of the grand tectonics of residential demography, without also viewing churches as living publics, as arenas of civic engagement, that can also instigate and resist those tectonics, fail to capture the real complexity of urban religious life.[5] Accounts that view churches only as potential saviors of the urban scene fall flat as well. Better to view organized religion as an integral part and producer of the urban scene, just as we do urban politics and urban economics.[6] The city is defined in part by its unique economic, demographic, and political forms; it should also be defined by its unique religious associational morphology. A step in this direction would be to revisit and update the core insights of the "urbanism" literature with religious institutions in mind. Originating with Louis Wirth's (1938) pivotal "Urbanism as a Way of Life" article, this thread of urban sociological thought conceptualized urban life in terms of the interactive and associational potential of the modern city. Of course, as Wirth speculated, there was the potential for a pandemic of emotional rootlessness and anomie. What is substantially more important for the work at hand, though, is that urbanism may also permit—even encourage—social orderliness, of creative synergy, of civic engagement, to congeal regularly in the city's apparently muddled soup of interpersonal encounters (Jacobs 1961; Lofland 1973; Duneier 1999). Alternatively, the city may be understood as a spaghetti of social networks, forming a complex system of subcultures, or *congregations*, each serving some community of affinity or circumstance (Fischer 1982, 1977). The important thing about the urbanism literature as it has developed since Wirth is that the urban civic order is understood as neither purely reactive nor purely agential. Urbanism is the ongoing response of individuals and collectives to the city, and it is the style and strategy of human attempts to shape urban life. It is not merely one or the other.

This core insight prevents us from arriving at unnecessarily shallow theories of why religious districts exist and how they impact the civic lives of their host neighborhoods. One well-worn theory of the density of churches in certain poor urban areas argues that the populations in those areas are looking for a way to escape their suffering. In that search, they turn in droves either to substances or spiritualities that remove them psychologically from the existential.[7] The religious district then is merely a pathological urban form, a symptom of poor people's pathological adaptation to urban life. Of course, it is difficult to imagine an essentially pathological form having a positive impact on local civic capacity.

The other theory regards the likely impact of the religious district on neighborhood social organization. It proclaims that churches, as entities *naturally* committed to community, moral order, and compassion, will be the organizational backbone of any neighborhood in which they are located. The churches will be the civic soul and the moral wit of those neighborhoods. They will protect and advocate for neighborhood children and families. Neighborhoods that contain many churches will therefore be particularly well served and should have no trouble organizing to get all kinds of resources to meet community needs. If churches fail to offer such nourishment, they appear not as symptoms of overall social and economic decline, but as empty distractions at best, and at worst as predators set on bamboozling their flocks (Frazier [1963] 1974; Myrdal 1944; DuBois [1899] 1996; Marx 1967).

For much of the rest of this chapter, I will review my alternative account of what this religious district phenomenon means. In this account, the religious district certainly appears as a product of or adaptation to bigger urban processes, but it is also an expression of moral order and civic agency on the part of religious people. That civic agency, in turn, is constrained by the institutional logic of the religious district itself. The religious district, then, is neither epiphenomenal nor purely agential. It is a living instance of civic life both reacting to and helping to create the broader urban environment.

Historical Emergence of a Compact and Diverse Religious Civic Form

Historically, the religious district phenomenon can be traced to the waves of black migration that pummeled the shores of northern urban centers in the first half of the twentieth century. Numerous urban sociologists since the time of the migration itself have observed how blacks were forcibly concentrated in overcrowded "black belt" areas during this period. But what is clear about early twentieth-century black Boston, as was clear about black belts all over the urban north, was that these black areas were not deeply homogenous but rather were diverse along many social dimensions. Voluntary associations, especially churches, made it possible for blacks to separate into distinct interest and affinity groups—whether black people from North Carolina or middle-class black Methodists from Virginia.

As a result, many churches might convene within fairly small geographic areas—Harlem, Bronzeville, Roxbury. Many of these churches were not large at all, but were small in membership, and only required a small amount of space, perhaps in a storefront situated on some major thoroughfare. During this period a new norm of religious practice emerged. This norm assumed that churches could locate quite near each other and not necessarily be in competition with each other over geographic territories; social distance, the differences between churches as social and cultural enclaves, not physical distance (as is the case with churches operating according to the parish model or template), could mediate competition. This is religion adapting to the urban process; it is religious people producing new forms of urban religious presence in response to the exigencies of mass migration and spatial segregation.

But this template presumed also that people felt comfortable shopping, in a sense, for the religious communities that suited their particular tastes. It assumed, in other words, that this was a voluntaristic religious context, where people could choose how and where to enact community.

Actually, there were writers already commenting on religious voluntarism and choice and shopping as a feature of religion in the United States in general, so this phenomenon was not one unique to black people. During this period Americans in general were witnessing the rise of forms of religious commitment that were not ascribed based on neighborhood or family but rather responded to individual preferences, social affinities, and a willingness to worship in places other than where one lived (Warner 1993).

After the midpoint of the century, when racist housing restrictions were relaxed and blacks began to pour into other parts of cities, this normative churchly template was reproduced in multiple parts of the city. These were the pockets of cities worst hit by the economic disinvestment that follows white flight and in some cases middle-class black flight (Wilson 1987). These pockets routinely contained dozens of vacant, cheaply rentable storefronts that nevertheless were unattractive to merchants because insurance was so high.

Churches move in and rent those spaces. After all, churches do not have to worry about competing with each other for residents of that particular neighborhood. If the church distinguishes itself demographically and culturally, people will commute from other parts of the city, and even from outside the city, to attend church where they feel most at home.

At any rate, contemporary religious districts like that in Four Corners are made possible by chronic economic depression but are sustained by the social distance between religious congregations, or what in the sociology of religion we call religious particularism. In other words, broader urban economic and demographic forces allow religious voluntarism, which is a national, cross-class, and cross-ethnic phenomenon, to crystallize in the unique form of the religious district.

Networks and Neighborhood Civic Life

As such, while the religious district may rightly be construed as a civically dense environment, it is possible only because it is a highly *fragmented* civic environment, with no intrinsically neighborhood-centered mission or membership base. From a neighborhood civic standpoint this matters because "place matters"; that is, neighborhoods continue to differ in terms of race and class composition, concentration of particular health problems, and crime rates (Sampson 1999; Jargowsky 1997; Massey 1996). Public and nonprofit community development programs tend to target discrete neighborhoods for grant making, and many municipal services are administered by local district. For this reason, neighborhoods persist as social units where collective action can, and often must, take place in defense of spatially bound interests. The question, then, is how religious organizations might make any difference in neighborhood collective action on behalf of the families who live there.

One way to approach this question is to consider the nature of the social networks that religious institutions build. If communication is the lifeblood, then social networks are the sinews of civic life. Theories of neighborhood social organization (specifically the systemic theoretical tradition originating with Morris Janowitz, adumbrated by Gerald Suttles, and updated recently by Robert Sampson in his collective efficacy studies) argue that institutions such as churches can foster collective action by building and participating in the civic networks that make such action possible. Neighborhood institutions are social spaces where interpersonal networks form; they are also corporate agents whose interorganizational networks can impact the collective quest for public goods (Sampson 1999). Connections among neighborhood institutions, what are called "horizontal" networks, help to coordinate and focus existing resources to address neighborhood problems (Kornhauser 1978; Pattillo 1998).

Connections between neighborhood institutions and institutions outside the neighborhood (such as social service agencies, foundations, and agents of the state), or "vertical networks," draw precious resources into the neighborhood while presenting neighborhood affairs to a broader public (Bursik and Grasmick 1993). When local institutions perform these vital networking functions, they form an "infrastructure" through which neighborhood concerns can be aired and addressed.

The emergence of such an infrastructure relies, of course, on whether churches and other institutions identify with the neighborhood in the first place. I found that churches perpetually built networks—among congregants, with other churches, and with vertically situated agencies. But recall that one main reason why religious districts can exist is because churches are not necessarily oriented toward the neighborhood in membership or mission. Churches thrive by carving out a social niche in the demographic and cultural landscape, not a neighborhood niche in the geographic landscape. In Four Corners, many pastors did not realize they were in a neighborhood called Four Corners. They knew that they had found a place to worship where rents were low and crime was high. This non-identification with the neighborhood was exacerbated by the fact that churches, like poor residents, were themselves highly mobile; when rents went up for whatever reason, churches, like people, were prone to leave for some other neighborhood. Church members who were used to traveling to worship simply followed the church. In addition, the perpetual threat of being "bounced" out of a neighborhood by impending economic development led some churches to actively avoid involvement in neighborhood affairs. They knew that revitalization would make them vulnerable, and they knew that people were cynical about their very presence in the neighborhood.

The network building that churches did engage in therefore tended to lack any neighborhood-focused purpose. Networks benefited church members, but not neighborhood residents. Interchurch networks were cross-neighborhood and citywide but remained thin within the neighborhood. Whatever "infrastructure" was emerging among these churches, then, was not brought to bear on neighborhood-level issues. Only two churches considered themselves neighborhood institutions, and these spearheaded, albeit haltingly, much of the revitalization work going on in the neighborhood. So the civic order that churches might have offered the neighborhood was actually projected outward and away from the neighborhood, because of the way the religious district, as an urban form, structured mission and membership.

Symbolic Boundaries and Civic Connections

So far I have only discussed the organizational forces and imperatives that make church identification with the immediate neighborhood and its civic concerns unlikely. This unlikelihood was only compounded by the inevitable encounters of churchgoers, most of whom lived elsewhere, with people and events in the street. I found that the street inevitably became a part of religious experience and identity in the churches by embodying notions of evil, providing sacred if dangerous opportunities to proselytize, and by providing sacred if dangerous opportunities to serve people in need. Street people were considered worthy of careful avoidance, conversion to "decent" churchly lifestyles, attentive service, or some combination of the latter two.[8]

One fairly well-known but highly exceptional Pentecostal church in Four Corners is an example of how a relatively *permeable* symbolic line between church and street permits the formation of civic connections, or social capital between the church world and street world. The Azusa Christian Community serves young people, mostly male, considered at risk of teetering into the criminal justice system. Although all of these services are operated under distinct 501c3s, Reverend Eugene Rivers, Azusa's founding pastor and the dynamo behind all of its social programs, sees social outreach as a matter of religious and community responsibility. His actual congregation remains quite small, composed of perhaps thirty people, in part because everyone is expected to participate heavily in the church's activist program. But Azusa's programs, run out of the Ella J. Baker House (literally a rehabilitated Victorian house), have reached hundreds of local people.

An emphasis on moral order is evident in the way the building is run. Everyone who enters—me, a semiretired beat police officer, an architect from London helping church members design a proposed science center—is asked to remove his or her hat, as are the young men who regularly circulate in the building. Cursing is strictly forbidden. Male staff members are required to wear neckties. By creating a highly ordered space, Azusa is able to offer its Ella J. Baker House as a "gang-neutral space" and "safe space" for young people trying to avoid trouble. Throughout any given day, young people are literally walking in off the street to take advantage of Azusa's tutoring and job placement services, or just to hang out.

Some of Azusa's programs directly incorporate secular activities that in many churches would be considered decadent or "street." For instance, in the safe space of the Baker House basement, young men hold boxing tournaments, which frequently serve to settle "beefs" between individuals and rival crews without resorting to armed struggle. It is the high level of moral order in the building that allows Azusa to metabolize "beef" into boxing without worrying about the fight escalating. "Nothing's gonna happen in here," Rivers once assured me. "No fights are going to break out in this church." Just that day, a teenager had broken house protocol by taking a couple of bare-fisted swings at his opponent, thus initiating an actual fight. Baker House staff pulled the two young men apart. I asked Rivers if this were not evidence of something "breaking out." "Here's how the religious piece comes in," he replied. "If this wasn't a church, [the initiator] would have got *mashed.*" In previous scuffles outside the church, the young man had "gotten his ass kicked." For taking advantage of the safe space, though, he was temporarily banished from Baker House.

The key here is that the individuals who frequent Baker House have *faith* in the stability of the order established by that community space. It is not that all have converted to Pentecostalism and joined Azusa, or that they have a generic respect for church buildings. It is a faith in the reality of order in *this* building, and a faith in Reverend Rivers and the younger mentors at the house, that propels the young men to socialize peacefully and maintain order among themselves. Rivers averred, "It's not a leap of faith, but a walk across a bridge built relationally"—that is, Rivers and his workers prove themselves trustworthy through ongoing relationships. And those relationships are initiated when church people cross the symbolic and physical line between church and street. Baker House regulars prove themselves trustworthy as well, over time. Furthermore, order is subtly and explicitly enforced, through everything from hats-off/neckties-on policies to temporary banishments.

To the extent that Baker House and similar programs are effective, it is probably because of the relationships of trust and mutual accountability—of *social faith*—they generate among participants. Of late, social scientists have referred to these kinds of relationships as "social capital," though the capital metaphor may be displaced, since these interpersonal matrices are not so much spent or invested, but *activated* for particular purposes. Religious people, particularly Protestant Christians, might broadly identify this as "fellowshipping": the ongoing, ever-deepening human interaction that makes congregants not simply a body of a faith, but an active community where people look after each other and are willing to hold each other to particular lifeways. In any case, this ordinary aspect of religious community generates precisely the kind of civic connection that scholars and policymakers operating in the savior mode expect to find.

But the great bulk of churches in Four Corners made sense of the street as an evil other, against which the church was defined. Again, many clergy were entirely unaware that they held church in a neighborhood called Four Corners. All knew that the streets were troubled and should be kept at arm's length. As I noted before, this idea of the church as wholly other, as being a world apart from the worst of the urban world, is not rare in religion, and the idea subtly motivates policies that view churches as ideal social service agencies. From a sociological standpoint, though, it appears that this set of churches, in defining itself as something entirely against the street, comes to *rely* on the street because the street world supplies the raw data about the nature of evil that gets incorporated into moral teaching. The fact of concentrated poverty and violence, which we can identify as an aspect of the urban environment, gives a particular flavor to the moral agency coming from churches. So the church and street ultimately are not separate here; yet the way that the street appears in the religious imagination discourages direct engagement with the immediate neighborhood. This further discourages many churches from becoming a part of neighborhood civic organization.

The religious communities that are most adept at fellowshipping, most skilled at generating internal social capital, may also require, *as a matter of spiritual survival*, that members avoid contact with people who have not committed their lives to the path of salvation. In the language of one of the more recent works on social capital (Putnam 2000), intimate "bonding" ties among church members can thwart the formation of "bridging" ties between churched and nonchurched. It is the bridging tie—the type of fellowshipping that deliberately leaps across the cognitive line between church and street—that might, for example, link a recently released prisoner to a religious community and its services. Azusa members made this leap because they thought of the street as a kind of social service area where the faithful were *supposed* to go to meet the material and social needs of marginalized persons, including ex-offenders. They were even willing to put aside explicit proselytizing to do so. But such religious communities cannot be taken as the norm.

Conclusion

What this means, first of all, is that we cannot reduce the religious district to our ordinary assumptions about why churches are in a place, and what churches are doing in and for the civic life of that place. We can see that the religious district is indeed a product of broader patterns of urban change, patterns of racial segregation, concentrated poverty, and economic underdevelopment, the likes of which are well studied in sociology. But it is also a product of people's diverse religious tastes and affinities, and their ability to shape and choose communities that reflect their view of where they fit in society and in the universe. In other words, the religious district is also a result of human agency that would give moral order to urban life, not just a knee-jerk adaptation to a dumb and merciless ecology. This self-organizing, purposive-congregating, meaning-generating activity gets at the heart of the moral order concept as it was used in the old Chicago school and as it was developed (largely without the semantic trappings of "moral order") in the urbanism literature.

But the moral orders that religious institutions and other institutions of civil society generate are conditioned, even limited, by their rootedness in the urban process. Religious districts endure over time because the churches in them have learned to survive by *not* focusing on their host neighborhoods in mission or membership. And again, this survival strategy developed as an adaptation to radical historical changes in black urban concentration and diversity. But as a result, we cannot assume that all of these churches are forming the backbone of a system of neighborhood social organization that will eventually save Four Corners, and neighborhoods like it, economically and socially. We cannot expect churches in religious districts to function as neighborhood institutions, as the civic soul of neighborhoods, because the moral order that these churches generate tends not to be oriented toward neighborhoods.

But rather than result in an indictment of churches, I hope this work will push research on poverty and civil society to examine more directly, and more deeply, the actual behaviors, inclinations, and limitations of institutions in neighborhoods. Based on my own research in this vein, I am compelled to offer, among other things, a counterpoint to all the excitement about "faith-based" community development and social services. Beneath much of this excitement is the assumption that churches really are neighborhood institutions—that they are inherently concerned with neighborhood affairs, that their clergy are in the streets making contact with neighborhood residents—and that churches, as quintessential neighborhood institutions, need only be contracted to do the work of secular nonprofits.

These assumptions deserve a good deal of interrogation, because churches, for some very common organizational and religious experiential reasons, are not necessarily anchors of neighborhood civic life. They are, however, anchors of *community* life—that is, the life of particular religious communities. By extension, the ongoing romance with neighborhoods as the ideal urban social units to which institutions and people should be civically attached, at least as a way of counteracting the causes and consequences of poverty, needs to be interrogated as well. This is the romance that motivates sociologists to look for the connection between neighborhood poverty and neighborhood social organization or the lack thereof. But neither disadvantage nor human community is necessarily confined to the contrived, sometimes fluctuating boundaries of local neighborhoods. It is the politics of urban resource distribution that identifies neighborhoods as primary civic units. I suggest that we cannot fully understand what churches might do as urban saviors, as contributors to the structural form and ideological content of urban civic life, until we understand how deeply churches are bound up in the urban process as a part and producer and product of that process, the same urban process whose by-products we find deeply troubling—the persistent poverty, the vast inequalities, the economic depression, the violence, the de facto political disenfranchisement, and so on. We should therefore examine the possible contradictions between this and the various orders envisioned by churches and other institutions of civil society. And we should consider how these possible disjunctions, rather than the mere absence or presence of local moral order, might contribute to persistent poverty and inequality.

Notes

1. Matthew 18:20, "For where two or three come together in my name, there am I with them."

2. Here I am alluding to Max Weber, who considered relationship to property a key dimension of class differentiation not only because some rented and others owned, but because people both signaled and reinforced class status by using property in different ways (Gerth and Mills 1958).

3. For more on the *meaning* of property and property usage in the construction of class and class interest, see Davis (1991) and Perin (1977).

4. The moral reformers preached that churches had to bring pastoral Christian values to the city to protect young urbanites from the brothels and saloons and reefer dens. The Social Gospellers, by contrast, wanted to inject Christian values of justice and social equality into oppressive industrial and political structures in the hope that this moral serum would induce permanent social reform and bring urbanites that much closer to the kingdom of God. See Boyer (1978).

5. For a full conceptualization of "public religion," see Jose Casanova (1994).

6. Several important exceptions form a thread through this tradition, where religious institutions are studied in their adaptive *and* agential modes. That thread begins with the work of St. Clair Drake (1940), continues through John Fish (1968), and culminates most recently in the work of Nancy Ammerman (1997), Gerald Gamm (1999), and McRoberts (2003). With this chapter I am attempting to identify this kind of analysis and raise its normative profile in the social scientific study of religion.

7. For example, see Ulf Hannerz (1969). Hannerz resonates clearly with Karl Marx, whose famous "opiate of the masses" statement suggested the religious agent's *desire* to become numb. Unlike Hannerz, though, Marx's formulation also implied the complicity of religious institutions in the perpetuation of capitalist oppression. Capitalists, in other words, used religion to control workers, just as workers used religion to soothe their pain.

Beyond Savior, Victim, and Sinner   97

8. This pattern echoes Elijah Anderson's (1999) findings regarding the way people distinguish decent ways of life from street ways of life. In one ethnography, Anderson was concerned with the interactions of blacks in a uniformly poor neighborhood. Not unlike churches that view the street world as an "evil other," Anderson's interviewees saw their neighbors as falling into two camps: "decent people" and "street people." Decent people were characterized by civility and dedication to work and family, while street people were associated with violence, public lewdness, personal and familial irresponsibility, joblessness, illicit activity, and proud nihilism. And, most important, those who considered themselves decent went out of their way to avoid those they associated with the street.

Works Cited

Ammerman, Nancy. 1997. *Congregation and Community*. New Brunswick, NJ: Rutgers.

———. 2002. "Connecting Mainline Protestant Congregations with Public Life." In *The Quiet Hand of God: Faith Based Activism and the Public Role of Mainline Protestantism*, Robert Wuthnow and John H. Evans, eds., 129–58. Berkeley: University of California Press.

Anderson, Elijah. 1999. *Code of the Street*. New York: W. W. Norton and Company.

Bennett, William J., John J. DiIulio Jr., and John P. Walters. 1996. *Body Count: Moral Poverty—and How to Win America's War Against Crime and Drugs*. New York: Simon and Schuster.

Boyer, Paul. 1978. *Urban Masses and Moral Order in America, 1820–1930*. Cambridge, MA: Harvard University Press.

Bursik, Robert J., and Harold Grasmick. 1993. *Neighborhoods and Crime: The Dimensions of Effective Community Control*. New York: Lexington.

Casanova, Jose. 1994. *Public Religions in the Modern World*. Chicago: University of Chicago Press.

Cnaan, Ram A. 2002. *The Invisible Caring Hand: American Congregations and the Provision of Welfare*. New York: New York University Press.

Davis, John Emmeus. 1991. *Contested Ground*. Ithaca: Cornell University Press.

Douglass, H. Paul. 1927. *Church in the Changing City*. New York: Doran.

Drake, St. Clair. 1940. *Churches and Voluntary Associations in the Chicago Negro Community*. Chicago: Works Projects Administration District 3.

DuBois, W. E. B. [1899] 1996. *The Philadelphia Negro*. Philadelphia: University of Pennsylvania Press.

Duneier, Mitchell. 1999. *Sidewalk*. New York: Farrar, Straus and Giroux.

Fischer, Claude. 1977. *Networks and Places: Social Relations in the Urban Setting*. New York: Free Press.

———. 1982. *To Dwell among Friends: Personal Networks in Town and City.* Chicago: University of Chicago Press.

Fish, John. 1968. *The Edge of the Ghetto: A Study of Church Involvement in Community Organization.* New York: Seabury Press.

Frazier, E. Franklin. [1963] 1974. *The Negro Church in America.* New York: Schocken Books.

Gamm, Gerald H. 1999. *Urban Exodus: Why the Jews Left Boston and the Catholics Stayed.* Cambridge, MA: Harvard University Press.

Gerth, H. H., and C. Wright Mills, eds. 1958. *From Max Weber: Essays in Sociology.* New York: Oxford University Press.

Hannerz, Ulf. 1969. *Soulside: Inquiries into Ghetto Culture and Community.* New York: Columbia University Press.

Jacobs, Jane. 1961. *The Death and Life of Great American Cities.* New York: Random House.

Jargowsky, Paul A. 1997. *Poverty and Place.* New York: Russell Sage Foundation.

Kincheloe, Samuel C. 1964. "Theoretical Perspectives for the Sociological Study of Religion in the City." *Review of Religious Research* 6:63–81.

Kornhauser, Ruth. 1978. *Social Sources of Delinquency.* Chicago: University of Chicago Press.

Levine, Donald N. 1995. *Visions of the Sociological Tradition.* Chicago: University of Chicago Press.

Lofland, Lyn. 1973. *A World of Strangers: Order and Action in Urban Public Space.* New York: Basic Books.

Marx, Gary T. 1967. "Religion: Opiate or Inspiration of Civil Rights Militancy among Negroes." *American Sociological Review* 32:64–72.

Massey, Douglas S. 1996. "The Age of Extremes: Concentrated Affluence and Poverty in the Twenty-First Century." *Demography* 33:395–412.

McRoberts, Omar. 2003. *Streets of Glory: Church and Community in a Black Urban Neighborhood.* Chicago: University of Chicago Press.

Myrdal, Gunnar. 1944. *An American Dilemma.* New York: Harper and Brothers.

Pattillo, Mary. 1998. "Sweet Mothers and Gang Bangers: Managing Crime in a Black Middle-Class Neighborhood." *Social Forces* 76:747–74.

Perin, Constance. 1977. *Everything in Its Place.* Princeton, NJ: Princeton University Press.

Putnam, Robert D. 2000. *Bowling Alone: The Collapse and Revival of American Community.* New York: Simon & Schuster.

Sampson, Robert. 1999. "What 'Community' Supplies." In *The Future of Community Development: A Social Science Synthesis,* Ronald F. Ferguson and William T. Dickens, eds., 241–92. Washington, DC: Brookings Institution Press.

Verba, Sidney, Kay Lehman Schlozman, and Henry E. Brady. 1995. *Voice and Equality: Civic Voluntarism in American Politics.* Cambridge, MA: Harvard University Press.

Warner, R. Stephen. 1993. "Work in Progress Toward a New Paradigm for the Sociological Study of Religion in the United States." *American Journal of Sociology* 98:1044–93.

Warren, Mark R. 2001. *Dry Bones Rattling: Community Building to Revitalize American Democracy.* Princeton, NJ: Princeton University Press.

Wilson, William J. 1987. *The Truly Disadvantaged: The Inner City, the Underclass, and Public Policy.* Chicago: University of Chicago Press.

Wirth, Louis. 1938. "Urbanism as a Way of Life." *American Journal of Sociology* 44:1–24.

Wood, Richard L. 2002. *Faith in Action: Religion, Race, and Democratic Organizing in America.* Chicago: University of Chicago Press.

6 How Religion Circulates in America's Local Public Square

Paul Lichterman

ALEXIS DE TOCQUEVILLE FAMOUSLY ARGUED THAT American religion would enhance American civic life. He imagined religion would promote concern for fellow humans and temper the passions that produce uncivil behavior. U.S. sociologists and political scientists have been rediscovering Tocqueville's writings amidst the news that American civic group memberships have declined steeply in the past thirty years (Putnam 2000). Many of them reiterate Tocqueville's paean to American religion. But how do people communicate religion in U.S. civic life today? How, if at all, does religion circulate in local civic organizations?

Social scientists and citizens alike often suppose—and it may seem obvious—that religion influences civic life through religious discourse. We often assume that religion is at work in public life if people talk God-talk and if they use religious rationales to defend their opinions. Scholars and citizens write about and worry about the effects of religious discourse on public conversation. Some wonder whether or not the United States has been engulfed in "culture wars" between religious and secular progressives on the one side and religious traditionalists on the other (Hunter 1991, 1994; DiMaggio et al. 1996; Williams 1997). Professional publicists and social movement leaders on both sides exchange fighting words over the right to an abortion, gay marriage, and other moral issues that have loomed large for several presidential elections. With just this sort of polarization in mind, some civil libertarians and liberal theorists say it would be best if people just kept religious discourse out of the public sphere. They suppose that religion makes public life irrational and that it is not a good basis for public reason.

On the other side, a variety of social scientists, policy scholars, and theologians—Theda Skocpol, Robert Putnam, Mary Jo Bane, Brent Coffin, Ronald Thiemann, Robert Bellah, and others—argue that religiously based community groups might potentially strengthen social ties in society at large.[1] None advocate that the United States become a "Christian nation." They argue that, given U.S. culture and history, there are widely shared religious traditions that would help people create social bonds. In a widely read commentary on religion in American life, social observer Richard John Neuhaus went so far as to call a public square without religion "naked" (1984). Concerned with the character of America's forums for public deliberation—its "public square"—Neuhaus claimed that a naked public square alienates many Americans who are prone to think in categories of religious belief and do not often distinguish sharply between moral and political spheres of action. From this standpoint, a public square that disallows statements of religious conviction is inauthentic, irrelevant, or—again—irrational to many Americans (see also Bellah et al. 1991).

Skeptics and promoters of public religion alike depict a public square in which citizens come armed with religious or antireligious *reasons* for their positions. They assume that religion influences civic life by giving us reasons we use to justify arguments and opinions. But is that how religion works in local voluntary associations?

My questions matter not only because voluntary civic associations matter, but because we need to understand better the place of religion in modern social and political life. Scholarship and daily news reports offer compelling critiques of the older modernist story of secularization, dominant until recently in sociology, that religion was becoming largely privatized in the United States (Luckmann 1967; Parsons 1967; Casanova 1994). No less a modernist intellectual than Jürgen Habermas considers the United States a "post-secular" society (2005). We do not have to be religious partisans or neoconservatives to wonder what ordinary Americans do with religious language in the local civic arenas that potentially host public discussion and build solidarities across diverse groups of people. Consider this recent statement:

> Misguided as some contemporary appeals to cramped versions of religious ideals may be, no one has yet found any substitute for the democratic energy unleashed historically by the best in America's tradition of Biblically inspired associationalism. (Skocpol 2000, 47)

The writer of this statement is neither a neoconservative nor a theologian, but sociologist Theda Skocpol. At the start of the new millennium, though, social scientists still did not understand so well the links between religious ideals and the democratic energy of civic engagement.[2] In light of popular understandings that (conservative) religion has swayed presidential elections and fragmented the United States into socially conservative "red" states and socially liberal "blue" states, the question is especially pressing.

Using two ethnographic examples of religious community service groups, this chapter investigates how religious language circulates in local voluntary associations in the United States. I suggest that when scholars equate public religion with religious deliberation about social issues, we miss important factors that shape the public influence or irrelevance of religious discourse. Members of local religiously based civic groups share distinct ideas about what it means to be a religious person, quite apart from their religious beliefs about the world. In both of the cases I will describe, shared notions of religious *identity* limited and even silenced religious *deliberation*. In these groups and perhaps others in the American civic arena, a "good" religious person was *not* someone who developed elaborate religious reasons for opinions on social issues.

The U.S. Case: Religious Disestablishment in the State, Religious Opportunity in Civil Society

There are good reasons to expect that religious deliberation *would* be widespread in the American local public square. First, given the sheer number of religiously sponsored civic groups in the United States and their breadth of activities, there are potentially many sites in which ordinary citizens talk in religious terms about social issues. Religiously based volunteer and advocacy groups have been prominent players in American community life from colonial times onward (Skocpol 2000; Thiemann et al. 2000). Almost half of Americans' association memberships are church related, and half of Americans' volunteering takes place in a religious context.[3] In the United States, religious organizations are rich, widespread sources of social networks that nurture volunteering and social activism.[4] Churches and synagogues are said to be the most widespread and egalitarian sites of civic engagement in the United States (Warner 1999, 238, derived from Ammerman 1997). These are sites in which even people of very modest social standing can learn the skills of organizing a meeting, debating public issues, or recruiting group members.

Religious commitments lead many Americans toward involvement with people and issues *beyond*, not just inside, their own congregations.[5] Religious congregations and networks of congregations house homeless adults and runaway teens, shelter battered women and children, serve hot meals to hungry people, donate clothing, and assist victims of natural disasters. They also advocate for cheaper housing, neighborhood development, environmental protection, educational opportunity, or gay and lesbian rights.[6] One might reasonably expect that members of these networks and civic alliances frequently discuss social issues in religious terms.

Of course, if we expect that religion must become more privatized (Luckmann 1967; Parsons 1967) along the lines of the classic secularization thesis that has shaped much of our sociological imagination about religion until recently, then we would not expect to hear much God-talk in the public square. Recent alternative frameworks, however, sharply revise those expectations. Sociologists Mark Chaves (1994) and Christian Smith (2003) have pointed out that secularization is a variable, contestable process, not an evolutionary universal, and may develop to different degrees in different segments of the same society. Individuals or distinct groups may hold strongly religious orientations even while the authority of religious institutions in a modern society at large diminishes relative to other institutions. Public religious deliberation could thrive in some local quarters of a social order that gives relatively little power to religious authorities. The "religious economy" perspective would come to a similar conclusion, though by a different route (Finke and Stark 1992; Warner 1993). It emphasizes that the U.S. Constitution's disestablishment of religion prepared the grounds for a vibrant "free market" in religious ideas. Rejecting the suppositions about rationality in sociology's old secularization thesis (and in the common-sense notions of some social elites), this perspective says there is little reason to assume that people should not be religious. Given the right enticements by eager "producers" of religious ideas, modern people may well "invest" in those ideas, affiliate with religious groups, and express themselves in religious terms. Neither of these perspectives assumes that religion must recede altogether from modern life outside the state.

Whatever the virtues in applying economic metaphors or retaining the "secularization" vocabulary, it is possible that religious discourse circulates in the civic arena of congregations, religious community service groups, and social movements, if not in arenas controlled by the state. Recent scholarship sees vivid religious symbolism and hears religious deliberation in community organizing outfits, peace activist groups, and local mobilizations against pornography (Wood 2002; Nepstad 2004; Hart 2001). If there are limits to religious deliberation in civic life after all, as I have found, those limits will be more broadly cultural than narrowly legal—matters of institutionalized expectation but not directly dictated by law or governmental policy.

Studying Religious Volunteer Groups in a Midwestern U.S. City

Following Religious Discourse in Two Local Groups

I discovered those cultural limits to religious deliberation in civic life during research for a book on religiously based voluntary associations (Lichterman 2005). For more than three years, I observed and participated in nine religiously based community service groups and projects in the midsize midwestern city of Lakeburg. I began the study just as welfare policy reform, described below, was taking effect in 1996. This chapter will focus on just two of the groups I followed. One of the groups, the Justice Task Force, developed a critical educational workshop about the politics of welfare reform and invited Lakeburg churches to host the workshop on Sundays before or after their weekly services. The other group, which I will call Adopt-a-Family, was a church volunteer group attached to a loose network of church groups. Each group in the Adopt-a-Family program committed itself to developing a supportive relationship with a former welfare-receiving family as the family breadwinner was making the transition from welfare to work.

I chose these and the other groups and projects in the larger study because they were good examples of voluntary civic associations, and they represent a variety of views within the Protestant religious majority in the United States. The Justice Task Force belonged to a theologically liberal Protestant association of churches that developed social service and educational programs and advocated on behalf of low-income people in Lakeburg. The Adopt-a-Family program belonged to a theologically conservative evangelical Protestant network of churches that initiated several community service and proselytization programs in Lakeburg. Groups in the Adopt-a-Family program itself were told not to proselytize the "adopted" families. During my study, I heard group members affirming that their purpose was not to "invite people to the

Kingdom of God" but to be compassionate servants or caring "neighbors" of the families they served.

While religious community service groups have long been central participants in the local public square, the welfare policy reforms of 1996 heightened these groups' public prominence. The "Charitable Choice" provision of the 1996 policy reforms requires government to consider religiously based groups when it contracts with organizations outside of government to provide social services. The Charitable Choice provision was supposed to encourage religious groups to apply for these contracts.[7] Some of the political rhetoric surrounding welfare reform and Charitable Choice coincided with the long-standing idea that religious faith promotes healthy social ties in America.[8] No single political position owns the idea: In the 2000 presidential race, candidates of both major parties endorsed an important role for local faith-based groups in the overall social contract with a shrunken federal government.

As an ethnographer, I listened closely to how members of each group discussed public issues. I scanned my field notes for evidence of members using religious language explicitly to legitimate opinions or lines of action. In which conversations, if any, did they use religious arguments? What I heard and recorded is interesting because at the time there were few studies that closely portrayed what ordinary conversation sounded like in religious voluntary associations.[9] The cases presented here will focus narrowly on conversation I heard about poverty or welfare policy. I want to point out what both sociological skeptics and sociological proponents of public religion have missed.

The Main Argument: A Puzzling Paucity of Religious Discourse

Proponents of public religious discourse such as R. J. Neuhaus or Robert Bellah have said that if religious deliberation is weak or nearly absent in public, it is either because religious Americans are somewhat confused and believe the public square *should* be religiously neutral, or else because many religious Americans today are incapable of reasoning in coherent religious terms at much length. Social critic Stephen Carter (1993) claimed that the major public institutions—law and education, for instance—stigmatize religious expression, contributing to the sense that religion may not belong in public discourse. Writers such as Neuhaus, Bellah, and Carter assume, then, that religious people do, or should, deliberate with religious rationales, and that if they do not it is because something external to religion stops them or else their own incapacities weaken them. My fieldwork in Lakeburg suggests, however, that the terms of the sociological discussion overemphasize the legitimating role of religious language and fail to understand religious communication in the group contexts of everyday life. Sociologists have made the mistake of treating civic life in America the way one might treat mass-mediated political life, where public spokespersons—especially conservative ones—use religious reasoning explicitly to make their case.

Ethnographic scenes from Lakeburg suggest to me, first, that the focus on religious deliberation about issues is out of step with the character of conversation in local religious civic groups. Deliberation with religious rationales may matter a lot less to religious people involved in local civic life than some academics and critics would think, hope, or fear. Second, I heard the religious groups imposing their own limits on religious discourse in subtle ways that the usual terms of debate about public religion cannot grasp. Borrowing Neuhaus's terms, we might say that religious group members colluded in creating a naked local public square. It was not just that outside institutions forced them to suppress religious reasoning or that members were incapable of speaking religious language; nor were they committed to an ideology of "neutrality" that would keep them from expressing their beliefs. They themselves limited the circulation of religious discourse even though they believed in religious reasons for their groups' goals.

While studies and critiques of public religion have focused on religious deliberation, my study found that more implicit aspects of religious personhood mattered a great deal in understanding how religious discourse circulates. The two groups studied here engaged in little religious deliberation because their ideal of the public religious person did not include sustained religious deliberation on public issues. To these group members, a religious person or group need not and perhaps ought not make lots of religious arguments. People who did, in their view, weren't ideal Christians. In fact, members of each group, in different ways, implicitly defined themselves against people who deliberate a great deal in religious terms. The Justice Task Force members figured such people put religion before justice either because they were Christian fundamentalists or else because they were overly polite "church people" who would rather trade in religious talk than political criticism. In Adopt-a-Family, sustained religious or secular argument would have sounded too "political" and therefore insufficiently compassionate or Christlike. Both groups saw sustained religious argumentation as the purview of professional experts or people with some form of religion-induced myopia—people either too close to or too distant from religion.

In short, group members' notion of religious *identity* kept them from wanting to use their religious *beliefs* to deliberate about social issues, even inside their own groups. The terms of sociological inquiry highlight either the dangers or the good of religious voices in a deliberative forum that the people I studied probably would not want to enter even if they could. It is not that they were committed to religious neutrality. It is that their way of being religious in public did not require a lot of elaborate religious reasoning.

Illustrations

Case One: Adopt-a-Family

The Adopt-a-Family program was a loose network of eight churches, mostly evangelical Protestant. Each of these churches sponsored a volunteer group of six to ten congregants, almost entirely white, mostly middle class, who were matched up with a former welfare-receiving family by a county social services agency. Most of the families were African American and lived in neighborhoods fifteen or twenty minutes away by car. The church groups made themselves available as practical and moral support groups for families whose breadwinners were looking for paid work given the new time limits on welfare payments from the state. Church group members helped out in all sorts of ways: They accompanied moms to appointments with doctors and social workers, went shopping at secondhand stores, bought telephone service, helped elder sons get driver's licenses, organized picnics with the families in the summertime. I followed two of the church groups, one very closely before it dissipated after seven months; examples in this section come from that group. In those seven months there were a mere three instances in which I heard members discuss, or *approach the possibility* of discussing, welfare policies from a religious point of view.

The first instance was at the program's orientation. At this three-hour meeting, the new church group volunteers were going to learn how to relate to members of their adopted families, how to make referrals if necessary, and how to find out about emergency resources if families ran out of money before the end of the month. Professionals from county family services, county housing services, Catholic Charities, and a Christian counseling center were there to teach the volunteers some very basic skills. Several of these professionals made their own evangelical Protestant identity explicit. The codirector said the volunteers would learn to practice Christlike care, serving the Lord by serving others. They were not to proselytize: "We're here to help, not to invite people into the Kingdom," as one church member put it later. They were not going to convert people, but there was no obvious reason they could not have developed Christian arguments about the new welfare policies had they wanted to.

Adopt-a-Family would not have existed were it not for welfare reform. Yet there was little talk about poverty or welfare policy. If anything, the orientation affirmed church group volunteers for staying out of the loop. The county housing official asked how many church volunteers knew whether or not the new welfare policies had taken effect yet. Some thought they had, some thought not. He responded, "See? We really don't know. It's confusing. It confuses me. This is how confusing the system is to be part of. I don't understand it all myself." He wasn't inviting the group members to deliberate about the policies that made the director dream up Adopt-a-Family to begin with. He was not inviting them to think as Christians about welfare reform. He was saying that the situation involved a lot of technicalities, and he was implying that the facts of the new policies weren't worth knowing. There wasn't any more discussion of it.

In the second potential opening for religious deliberation, at a meeting of church group leaders a few weeks later, I heard the director exchange a few quick, barely audible words with one of the group leaders. The director was saying that there were "issues to be knowledgeable about" regarding a "terrible choice." I puzzled over what was so "terrible," and while typing up my field notes, I realized that I had heard him incorrectly. In the context of this discussion, he must have said not "terrible choice" but "Charitable Choice"—the name given to part of the 1996 welfare legislation that encourages religious organizations to apply for government grants to run social service programs. Recipients of welfare assistance could choose church-run social services (the "Charitable Choice") instead of programs run by government agencies. No one else at the meeting said anything about the Charitable Choice provisions in the new welfare policies. Given my own misinterpretation, it is likely no one even *heard* anything about them; the point is that this was hardly a forum for applying religious beliefs to public policies.

In the third instance, two months later, a local research institute sent a pack of quizzes—little tests with correct answers printed on the back—to Adopt-a-Family's director. The director passed them on to church group leaders. Members of the group I was studying took the quiz during a meeting. The quiz was supposed to correct common misperceptions. People who took it would learn, for instance, that the average number of children in a welfare-receiving family was only 1.9; Americans commonly think that families receive welfare assistance because they are irresponsible and bring many children into the world without the financial means to support them (see Hays 2003). The group read through the correct answers on the back of the quiz sheets when they were finished.

It was a remarkably quiet exercise, even in this normally gregarious group. If ever there was an opportunity for deliberating about social issues in religious terms, this should have been it. The single bit of plausibly religious language I heard during this whole session emerged when one member guessed the wrong answer to the question of how much money an average welfare recipient receives. She said, "I guess I overestimated the compassion of the government." Only one of the ten quiz questions elicited any back-and-forth dialogue at all, beyond such single-sentence commentaries as "Oh, I didn't know that." The conversation-starting question was about the causes of poverty. The lead participant in this brief exchange was a woman who said she'd heard on the radio that there would be no poverty if everyone followed two principles: "Don't quit a job until you have another one, and don't spend more money than you have coming in." "That's it?" she asked rhetorically. "I thought it would be something deeper." While the group certainly did talk about its adopted family's particular circumstances, this was the longest exchange I ever heard on poverty and welfare as *public issues*. Religious discourse entered only very briefly and subtly, when the one member said she overestimated the government's "compassion."

Scholars and social critics often take religious deliberation as the measure of religion's influence in public. Yet researchers have been finding that American volunteer groups do not discuss public issues in the deliberate, citizenly terms that Tocquevillians or other civil society theorists might expect. In these very widespread civic groups, political conversation often is considered impolite, a threat to the upbeat, task-oriented sensibility that defines "volunteering" in stark contrast with "politics" for many Americans (see Eliasoph 1998; Wuthnow 1991).

I was struck by the lack of religious deliberation on welfare reform in an explicitly Christian group whose very existence depended on the policy change. After all, these evangelical Protestants were good at talking about their religious faith with friends and strangers alike—including the participant-observer—and applying the teachings of Jesus to everyday events. Group members referred to the example of Jesus as they were planning what to do with their adopted family and as they were talking about the risks they were taking to make contact with people very different from them. They opened and sometimes closed meetings with prayer. In these ways we might say they were legitimating their group in explicitly Christian terms. They certainly were not incapable of thinking about their tasks in religious terms, but they were not deliberating with religious rationales either.

It would be hard to say that the state restricted the group's religious expression. The Lakeburg county agency that selected willing families for Adopt-a-Family's program knew that Adopt-a-Family was a Christian group and made sure that potential families knew what they were "choosing" if they decided to participate in the program. County social workers had said these were new times and that the "door was open" now for work with explicitly religious groups that public agencies would not have worked with before welfare reform. Furthermore, group members did not accept an ideology of religious neutrality as Neuhaus might fear: They always said that government agencies and community groups needed to accept them as a specifically Christian group. They were not going to sidestep their religious identity for public purposes. So why wasn't this group more of a forum for religious deliberation?

To academic outsiders, it might seem as if group members were stepping into history, supporting the new social contract with old-fashioned Protestant notions of voluntary charity and hard work. But that is not how group members saw it. A good Christian, in public, was a "social servant"—an individual who touches people heart-to-heart in a world of individual hearts, not a historical actor or a deliberator. As I explain at length elsewhere (Lichterman 2005; Eliasoph and Lichterman 2003), groups have enduring ways of understanding their identities on a wider social map. They have powerful social identities, that is, and I discovered that servanthood is one such identity. Servanthood carries particular customs regarding what can be said, and what must not be said, on a variety of topics. Violating the customs of servanthood or any other social identity would threaten a group's own togetherness and shut down discussion.

In the case of Adopt-a-Family, volunteers defined their social identity in sharp contrast with bureaucratic service agencies and people who talk in abstractions. As the county housing official (himself an evangelical) put it, group members might "assess needs" of their adopted families—not the way social workers do, but more the way a discerning, caring, Christlike servant would. When the church group I followed closely decided to collect clothes for their family's newborn, they said, "We're doing this as a friendship thing. It's not just a new kind of welfare." "We're not just another government program," stated one member. As the group leader said, "We're not experts; thank God we don't have to have all the answers." And Adopt-a-Family's director criticized people who *talk* a lot about social issues in systematic terms, engaging in abstractions while individuals are hurting. The message was clear: "People like us" don't engage in abstract discussion; we care and we help. The (evangelical) director once even criticized a local association of evangelical pastors for spending time circulating a Christian position on gay marriage. The association was getting involved in "politics" instead of doing what Christians ought to do.

Experts deliberate, assess, and write position statements. Servants empathize, nurture, and try to do what Jesus would do for the served. As social servants, Adopt-a-Family privileged discernment, not deliberation. The director was all for public talk of a sort: public praying. He organized a "concert of prayer" in a Lakeburg sports arena. But speaking up as religious people in public *debate* about issues was, in his words, tiresome, a burnout.

R. J. Neuhaus argued that many ordinary Americans are alienated from the public square because they have to leave their religious beliefs at the door. He figured that was why the Christian political right seemed to be gaining so much ground when he wrote in the 1980s—conservative Christians in public talked God-talk, or values-talk, at length. Contemporary political commentators use the same rationale to explain why Democratic Party candidates lose to Republicans in national elections; the reelection of President George W. Bush in 2004 by a narrow margin is a case in point. But the ordinary evangelicals in my study didn't seem eager to propound their religious beliefs in deliberation. The scenario described above suggests that this was not because they were invested in welfare reform and afraid to hear criticisms of the new policies. Rather, they did not express much interest in having a developed opinion on the policies at all. Possibly they enjoyed hearing *others*—national leaders—identifying as Christians in public. But I got little sense that they themselves would want to participate in religious deliberation. For social servants, the public square is inauthentic from the start. Real Christians are elsewhere, off the historical map. The terms of Neuhaus's feisty indictment of public life miss this social reality.

Case Two: Justice Task Force

My other illustrations come from a different kind of civic association with a more self-consciously political imagination. Late in 1995 a loose network of fifty Lakeburg churches started to organize some emergency safety-net projects as a response to the upcoming welfare reforms. Longtime participants in this urban religious network feared the worst consequences of the new regulations, imagined many former welfare recipients would go hungry and homeless, and felt compelled to do something. Some of them formed the Justice Task Force, a kind of education and agitation group that met monthly. The task force drew mainly from theologically liberal, mainline Protestant churches, with a couple of Catholic members too—all white, of mostly professional backgrounds—with roughly ten core members and several dozen more who had come to a meeting or received the group's mailings. The task force put together an educational workshop called The Growing Divide, and they hoped to present the workshop in many local churches.

This group, unlike the Adopt-a-Family group, was very much about deliberation of a sort. The Growing Divide workshops could have been just the place to cultivate a religious voice, a quite different voice, on the issues that Adopt-a-Family had tried to transcend on their way to Christlike care. Task force meetings often became what social theorists would call a site of the public sphere (Habermas 1989; Taylor 1995), a forum where public-spirited conversation could flow freely. Many times a forum would spring up spontaneously in the midst of a meeting: Members would break into fast and furious discussion—about the growing income gap in the United States and about the failure of local banks to send some of their mortgage servicing fees to a fund for homeless shelters, the way a new state law required. It wasn't deliberation in the even-handed, explore-all-viewpoints, liberal model; it was more like what political theorist Nancy Fraser (1992) might call a subaltern public, a forum that cultivates a critical viewpoint.

Sometimes religious rationales entered the forum, usually as brief references. At one meeting, the group's leader said, "As people of faith, we need to bring in some of the injustice language from the Hebrew and Christian Bibles." And she enumerated some phrases quickly, one after the other: "'He will punish and avenge the wrongs people suffer,' 'listen to the reapers,' and 'justice, mercy, honesty, these you should follow.'" She said, "This is judgmental language, but we say we're people of the Book; we believe this stuff, but we don't do it."

I went to several of the Growing Divide workshops. At two of them, religious language was not obviously in evidence at all: There was hearty critique of the injustice that gives corporate executives dozens of times more income than average workers, but no explicitly religious discussion of the fact. When I walked into the church classroom where one workshop was being held, I saw the walls lined with construction paper placards, each one quoting a biblical passage that could support the workshop's social critique. A task force member had gotten a Bible on computer disc and printed the results of a search she had run on justice-related biblical passages. The paper placards bore silent witness to Judeo-Christian imperatives, but no one *discussed* them during the workshop.

In the task force, members wore their religious identities in a particular way: They related to religious rationales as resources to justify points of view that they developed at much greater length in the group in *secular* language. That is how religious discourse circulated in this group and its workshops—as a kind of supplementary motif for the main show.

Many meetings might go by without any religious language at all. But almost every meeting rang with critical ideology that came from other educational workshops or from works of social criticism that members were reading. One night twelve of us sat around the table and listened as one member spoke for over an hour on corporate neoliberalism and its global consequences. It was a longer version of the same themes we had heard many times in the previous two years. A locally well-known radical radio talk-show host had come to the meeting that night. I figured he'd find this a congenial place to be. Yet he sat silently for a long time, and finally he told us in a rising voice that he represented "a race [African American] that doesn't live as long. . . . There are lots of Blacks who don't care a lot about ideology." He thought the group should be able to "act on [its] faith underpinnings." He must have thought that religious rationales could secure those underpinnings more effectively than the secular analysis he'd been hearing for an hour. At last he blurted out, "We know who the number-one activist is, the one who risked everything—JESUS!" Quickly he qualified himself: "That's my belief anyway." No one else spoke up for Jesus or for religious faith of any sort. The radio announcer didn't come back to another meeting.

During two years of meetings, I did hear leading members say a number of times that they should have a session in which people would *talk about* the religious bases of their positions. They scheduled such a meeting on the group

agenda several times. The group never got around to that religious deliberation session in the two years that I followed them.

I slowly gathered that religious deliberation was not the preferred mode of
speaking. Why was that? Again, groups have enduring ways of understanding
their identities on a wider social map. The task force took on what I call a
"social critic" identity, one they share with many other U.S. citizen groups,
religious and secular. On their social critics' social map, there were many reference points *against* which the group defined itself: greedy corporations,
complacent media, and largest of all, conventional church people. "Church
people" was a reference point *against* which task force members identified
themselves, just as governmental social service represented a reference point
against which Adopt-a-Family defined its own version of the publicly engaged
Christian. Task force members disparaged "church people" as people who
stand for charity, ignore calls for justice, and try to be polite and agreeable. In
members' perceptions, their Lakeburg church congregations were filled
mostly with polite, socially myopic people who wanted to give charity but not
do justice.

The social critic identity came with customary norms of speech and action, different from those of social servants. To speak at length in religious
terms would be to risk being identified with "church people" who stand on
the wrong side of the fence. Speaking that way, in other words, would violate
the group's own solidarity. In task force members' perception, one could be
either mostly secular and critical or else mostly religious and meliorist, and
they preferred the first to the second. So the task force welcomed one new
participant who equated religious people with fundamentalists. Yet it was
unwelcoming toward church people who came to meetings and didn't participate readily in the group's many solidarity-building jokes and ironic stories about corporations and government officials. The group was chilly even
toward people who were critical of welfare reform but didn't have quite the
same critical style of self-presentation. The identity itself mattered, apart
from beliefs about welfare, poverty, or justice.

At least some task force members belonged to churches whose national
denominational offices would have distributed position papers critical of
welfare privatization. Yet in two years of meetings, I never heard people talking about such church-based sources. A member once mentioned that a
congress of U.S. Catholic bishops had written critically on social issues (the
member wasn't Catholic herself), but the comment went nowhere. Church-

based sources were suspect. Though they attended churches regularly, task force members did not wish to speak or hear a lot of *religious* discourse in a deliberative forum.

In both the Justice Task Force and Adopt-a-Family, implicit notions of religious *identity* constrained members' use of religious language, even in groups whose members all attended church. These implicit but powerful social identities need to be part of the debate about why and how religious deliberation emerges in the public square. Elsewhere I treat the larger cultural and institutional sources of these identities, but I emphasize here that the groups constructed these identities for themselves; they were not simply foisted on the groups by antireligious institutions or dominant secular ideologies. While there may be a "free market" in religious ideas as religious economy theorists say, these cases suggest there are strong cultural constraints on how the "buyers" and "sellers" of public religion use religious discourse.

To understand how religious discourse circulates in civic life, it is not enough to think religious deliberation emerges wherever there are religious people who are free to deliberate about social issues. In order to understand the cultural tissue of the group settings in which people speak, we need to listen closely and investigate those settings. Local civic group settings are not the same as the often mass-mediated settings of political debate, where interest group leaders hurl religious or antireligious salvos at one another. Different settings carry very different expectations about identity, as well as different expectations about who is a worthwhile speaker and what kind of speech is appropriate (Eliasoph and Lichterman 2003).

Conclusion

The two cases described in this chapter can only begin to suggest larger patterns of religious discourse in local U.S. civic life. However, it is striking that theologically liberal and conservative Protestants, quite often different in their political as well as religious beliefs, shared a similar understanding that religious deliberation is not what a good Christian does in the local public square, despite the hopes of some academics, critics, and theologians. Particular settings elicit distinct norms of religious communication, even in a society with high rates of religious participation. Religious communication in local civic life, the local public square, may not sound the same or follow the same rules as religious communication in mass-mediated forums or state-sponsored arenas.

To study religion's public roles, we need to get beyond the common emphasis on beliefs and rationales in the abstract. It seems safe to say religious teachings *did* matter to members of both groups. They did not have to mention "the justice language of the Hebrew and Christian Bibles" or "what Jesus would do" at all if they did not want to. They did not have to identify explicitly as religious groups rather than as groups that happened to be made up of churchgoers. Some community volunteers from churches in my larger study (Lichterman 2005) never identified as religious people while volunteering. The limited empirical material here is enough to make the case that scholars can benefit by investigating ordinary people's ways of communicating religion in public. One would need many more than two cases, with tricky comparisons between religiously and nonreligiously identified groups, to make causal claims about religion's effects on community service groups. But there are other things these cases can start to teach us about how people live with religion and what it means to be religious in public. We benefit by switching from the usual question of how religion affects people to the question of what people do with religion.

Understanding what people do with religion in civic life, how they "wear" it, is particularly pressing in a time of institutional restructuring. Cultural understandings of religious identity will not change automatically when laws or institutional relationships change. Public institutions did change in Lakeburg: The director of Adopt-a-Family said many times that he appreciated the "new openness" that local state agencies were showing religious groups after welfare reform. These agencies were not handing over social services to religious groups, but they were suggesting the possibility of new, not well-specified forms of collaboration. New institutional arrangements could motivate deliberation; religious groups might want to develop religious reasons for participating in new relationships with welfare agencies. But the "new openness" on the part of the state did not motivate much public religious discourse in the civic groups I studied. Customary notions of religious identity—the idea that a truly good Christian does not deliberate in Christian terms—remained powerful. These customary understandings are something like "institutions" themselves in the sense that neo-institutionalists use the term (Becker 1999; Armstrong 2002; DiMaggio et al. 1991). They have their own histories and their own power over what people can say, to whom, and where. Ironically, and counter to the fears of well-intentioned critics, the government's embrace of local religious groups does little to empower religious reasoning unless the groups develop different ideas about what it means to have a religious identity in public. In the two groups described here, religious identity kept religious faith from developing a stronger voice even inside the groups themselves.

People who would like to link humane religious values more closely to public policy will have to innovate new ways of presenting religious identity in public. The anti–public servant and the self-marginalizing social critic pictured here do not help religious teachings make their way into broad public debate. People who speak from either of these identities end up sequestering religious teachings in tiny spaces or else severing them from the historical, political world altogether. Meanwhile, research suggests that the most widely known model of public religious identity in the United States—embodied in the fiery, conservative Christian spokesperson—is unsavory or just irrelevant to many Americans, including quite a number of theological conservatives (Smith 1998, 2000). Several Justice Task Force members told me they did not want to talk about their religious reasons for being in the task force because "Christian fundamentalists talk that way." A self-perpetuating cycle may take shape: If people do not experiment with new ways of presenting religious identity in local forums, it becomes that much easier to assume that sounding religious in public is something only Christian conservatives on television do. In effect, these assumptions increase the power of Christian conservatives to define what it means to be religious in public at all. If the post-secularist understanding of modern American religion is correct, then religious discourse will not disappear from public life anytime soon. Sociologists will better understand religion's public potential and danger in a post-secular society if we get beyond beliefs and pay more attention to identities and settings for religious communication.

Notes

This chapter was first published in Paul Lichterman, "Circulation de la religion sur la place publique locale aux Etats-Unis," *Sociologie et sociétés* 38, no. 1 (Spring 2006): 31–53.

1. See Skocpol (2000), Robert Putnam (2000, especially 408–10), Bane and Coffin (2000), Coffin (2000), Thiemann et al. (2000), Bellah et al. (1991, 1985); see also Bell (1976).

2. See Wuthnow's (1999) comments on the point.

3. See Putnam (2000), p. 66, and chapter 4 in general.

4. See Becker and Dhingra (2001); Park and Smith (2000); Putnam (2000); Wilson (2000); Greeley (1997); Wuthnow (1991, 1998); Verba, Schlozman, and Brady (1995); Wood (1999, 2002); Mark R. Warren (2001); Chaves, Giesel, and Tsitsos (2002).

5. For instance, Greeley (1997); Putnam (2000); Verba, Schlozman, and Brady (1995); Wuthnow et al. (1990); Eckstein (2001); Wilson and Musick (1997); but see Wilson (2000).

6. See Ammerman (2002), Thiemann et al. (2000), Mark R. Warren (2001), Wood (1999, 2002); see also Demerath and Williams (1992).

7. See helpful discussions in Chaves (1999), Greenberg (2000), and Bartkowski and Regis (2003).

8. As one of his first domestic policy initiatives, President George W. Bush established a federal Office of Faith-Based and Community Initiatives. When John DiIulio, former head of the office, described the mission of this initiative, he argued that local faith-based social service groups could strengthen social bonds: "We've become habituated to transacting our moral and social responsibility for the welfare of others through distant others," he said. Instead of helping one another, Americans push one another away, weakening the bonds of interdependence. DiIulio implied that faith-based groups could strengthen those bonds and make ordinary citizens more responsible for the fabric of society. The quote and paraphrased statement come from John DiIulio's lecture in the John M. Olin Foundation Lectures on the Moral Foundations of American Democracy, Princeton University, April 27, 2001. The synopsis of his lecture is available at www.princeton.edu/webannounce/Princeton_Headlines/Archived/2001/APR_Text.html.

9. Since then, a few similar studies have emerged. See Richard Wood's (2002) study of local religiously based advocacy groups for low-income people in California, Jerome Baggett's (2000) study of a religious voluntary association whose members build inexpensive homes for low-income people, or Dawne Moon's (2004) study of debates over homosexuality in Methodist churches in the Midwest.

Works Cited

Ammerman, Nancy. 1997. *Congregation and Community.* New Brunswick, NJ: Rutgers University Press.

———. 2002. "Connecting Mainline Protestant Churches with Public Life." In *The Quiet Hand of God: Faith-Based Activism and the Public Role of Mainline Protestantism,* Robert Wuthnow and John Evans, eds., 129–58. Berkeley: University of California Press.

Armstrong, Elizabeth. 2002. *Forging Gay Identities.* Chicago: University of Chicago Press.

Baggett, Jerome. 2000. *Habitat for Humanity: Building Private Homes, Building Public Religion.* Philadelphia: Temple University Press.

Bane, Mary Jo, and Brent Coffin. 2000. "Introduction." In *Who Will Provide? The Changing Role of Religion in American Social Welfare*, Mary Jo Bane, Brent Coffin, and Ronald Thiemann, eds., 1–20. Boulder CO: Westview Press.

Bartkowski, John, and Helen Regis. 2003. *Charitable Choices: Religion, Race and Poverty in the Post-Welfare Era*. New York: New York University Press.

Becker, Penny Edgell. 1999. *Congregations in Conflict*. Cambridge and New York: Cambridge University Press.

Becker, Penny Edgell, and P. H. Dhingra. 2001. "Religious Involvement and Volunteering: Implications for Civil Society." *Sociology of Religion* 62:315–36.

Bell, Daniel. 1976. *The Cultural Contradictions of Capitalism*. New York: Basic Books.

Bellah, Robert, Richard Madsen, William Sullivan, Ann Swidler, and Steven Tipton. 1985. *Habits of the Heart: Individualism and Commitment in American Life*. Berkeley: University of California Press.

———. 1991. *The Good Society*. New York: Alfred Knopf.

Berman, Sheri. 1997. "Civil Society and the Collapse of the Weimar Republic." *World Politics* 49:401–29.

Boyte, Harry, and Sara M. Evans. 1986. *Free Spaces: The Sources of Democratic Change in America*. New York: Harper & Row.

Carter, Stephen. 1993. *The Culture of Disbelief*. New York: Basic Books.

Casanova, Jose. 1994. *Public Religions in the Modern World*. Chicago: University of Chicago Press.

Chaves, Mark. 1994. "Secularization as Declining Religious Authority." *Social Forces* 72:749–75.

———. 1999. "Religious Congregations and Welfare Reform: Who Will Take Advantage of 'Charitable Choice'?" *American Sociological Review* 64:836–46.

Chaves, Mark, Helen Giesel, and William Tsitsos. 2002. "Religious Variations in Public Presence: Evidence from the National Congregations Study." In *The Quiet Hand of God: Faith-Based Activism and the Public Role of Mainline Protestantism*, Robert Wuthnow and John Evans, eds., 108–28. Berkeley: University of California Press.

Coffin, Brent. 2000. "Where Religion and Public Values Meet: Who Will Contest?" In *Who Will Provide? The Changing Role of Religion in American Social Welfare*, Mary Jo Bane, Brent Coffin, and Ronald Thiemann, eds., 121–43. Boulder, CO: Westview Press.

Demerath, N. J., and Rhys Williams. 1992. *A Bridging of Faiths: Religion and Politics in a New England City*. Princeton, NJ: Princeton University Press.

DiMaggio, Paul, Bethany Bryson, and John Evans. 1996. "Have Americans' Social Attitudes Become More Polarized?" *American Journal of Sociology* 102:690–755.

DiMaggio, Paul, John Evans, Bethany Bryson, and Walter Powell, eds. 1991. *The New Institutionalism in Organizational Analysis*. Chicago: University of Chicago Press.

Eckstein, Susan. 2001. "Community as Gift-Giving: Collectivistic Roots of Volunteerism." *American Sociological Review* 66:829–51.

Eliasoph, Nina. 1998. *Avoiding Politics: How Americans Produce Apathy in Everyday Life.* New York: Cambridge University Press.

Eliasoph, Nina, and Paul Lichterman. 2003. "Culture in Interaction." *American Journal of Sociology* 108:735–94.

Finke, Roger, and Rodney Stark. 1992. *The Churching of America, 1776–1990: Winners and Losers in Our Religious Economy.* New Brunswick, NJ: Rutgers University Press.

Fraser, Nancy. 1992. "Rethinking the Public Sphere: A Contribution to the Critique of Actually Existing Democracy." In *Habermas and the Public Sphere,* Craig Calhoun, ed., 109–42. Cambridge, MA: MIT Press.

Greeley, Andrew. 1997. "Coleman Revisited: Religious Structures as a Source of Social Capital." *American Behavioral Scientist* 40 (March–April):587–94.

Greenberg, Anna. 2000. "Doing Whose Work? Faith-Based Organizations and Government Partnerships." In *Who Will Provide? The Changing Role of Religion in American Social Welfare,* Ronald Thiemann, Mary Jo Bane, and Brent Coffin, eds., 178–97. Boulder, CO: Westview Press.

Habermas, Jürgen. 1989. *The Structural Transformation of the Public Sphere.* Cambridge, MA: MIT Press.

———. 2005. "Religion in the Public Sphere." Lecture presented at the Fourth Annual Kyoto Laureate Symposium, University of San Diego, March 4.

Hart, Stephen. 2001. *Cultural Dilemmas of Progressive Politics.* Chicago: University of Chicago Press.

Hays, Sharon. 2003. *Flat Broke with Children.* New York: Oxford University Press.

Hunter, James D. 1991. *Culture Wars: The Struggle to Define America.* New York: Basic Books.

———. 1994. *Before the Shooting Begins: Searching for Democracy in America's Culture War.* New York: Free Press.

Lichterman, Paul. 2005. *Elusive Togetherness: Church Groups Trying to Bridge America's Divisions.* Princeton, NJ: Princeton University Press.

Luckmann, Thomas. 1967. *The Invisible Religion: The Problem of Religion in Modern Society.* New York: Macmillan.

Moon, Dawne. 2004. *God, Sex, and Politics: Homosexuality and Everyday Theologies.* Chicago: University of Chicago Press.

Nepstad, Sharon. 2004. *Convictions of the Soul.* New York: Oxford University Press.

Neuhaus, Richard J. 1984. *The Naked Public Square: Religion and Democracy in America.* Grand Rapids, MI: Eerdmans Publishing.

Park, J. Z., and C. Smith. 2000. " 'To Whom Much Has Been Given . . .': Religious Capital and Community Voluntarism among Churchgoing Protestants." *Journal for the Scientific Study of Religion* 39:272–86.

Parsons, Talcott. 1967. *Sociological Theory and Modern Society*. New York: The Free Press.

Putnam, Robert. 2000. *Bowling Alone: The Collapse and Revival of American Community*. New York: Simon and Schuster.

Skocpol, Theda. 2000. "Religion, Civil Society, and Social Provision in the U.S." In *Who Will Provide? The Changing Role of Religion in American Social Welfare*, Mary Jo Bane, Brent Coffin, and Ronald Thiemann, eds., 21–50. Boulder, CO: Westview Press.

Smith, Christian. 1998. *American Evangelicalism: Embattled and Thriving*. Chicago: University of Chicago Press.

———. 2000. *Christian America? What Evangelicals Really Want*. Berkeley: University of California Press.

———. 2003. "Introduction: Rethinking the Secularization of American Public Life." In *The Secularization Revolution*, Christian Smith, ed., 1–96. Berkeley: University of California Press.

Taylor, Charles. 1995. "Liberal Politics and the Public Sphere." In *New Communitarian Thinking*, Amitai Etzioni, ed., 183–217. Charlottesville: University Press of Virginia.

Thiemann, Ronald, Samuel Herring, and Betsy Perabo. 2000. "Risks and Responsibilities for Faith-Based Organizations." In *Who Will Provide? The Changing Role of Religion in American Social Welfare*, Mary Jo Bane, Brent Coffin, and Ronald Thiemann, eds., 51–70. Boulder, CO: Westview Press.

Verba, Sidney, Kay Schlozman, and Henry Brady. 1995. *Voice and Equality: Civic Voluntarism in American Politics*. Cambridge, MA: Harvard University Press.

Warner, R. Stephen. 1993. "Work in Progress Toward a New Paradigm for the Sociological Study of Religion in the United States." *American Journal of Sociology* 98:1044–93.

———. 1999. "Changes in the Civic Role of Religion." In *Diversity and Its Discontents*, Neil Smelser and Jeffrey Alexander, eds., 229–43. Princeton, NJ: Princeton University Press.

Warren, Mark R. 2001. *Dry Bones Rattling: Community Building to Revitalize American Democracy*. Princeton, NJ: Princeton University Press.

Williams, Rhys, ed. 1997. *Culture Wars in American Politics*. New York: Aldine de Gruyter.

Wilson, John. 2000. "Volunteering." *Annual Review of Sociology* 26:215–40.

Wilson, John, and Marc Musick. 1997. "Toward an Integrated Theory of Volunteering." *American Sociological Review* 62:694–713.

Wood, Richard L. 1999. "Religious Culture and Political Action." *Sociological Theory* 17:307–32.

———. 2002. *Faith in Action: Religion, Race and Democratic Organizing in America*. Chicago: University of Chicago Press.

Wuthnow, Robert. 1991. *Acts of Compassion*. Princeton, NJ: Princeton University Press.

————. 1998. *Loose Connections: Joining Together in America's Fragmented Communities.* Cambridge, MA: Harvard University Press.

————. 1999. "Mobilizing Civic Engagement: The Changing Impact of Religious Involvement." In *Civic Engagement in American Democracy,* Theda Skocpol and Morris Fiorina, eds., 331–63. Washington, DC, and New York: Brookings Institution Press and Russell Sage Foundation.

Wuthnow, Robert, Virginia Hodgkinson, and Associates. 1990. *Faith and Philanthropy in America.* San Francisco: Jossey-Bass.

7

A Tacit Sense of Evil? The Meaning of Politics in United Methodist Debates over Homosexuality

Dawne Moon

A KEY ELEMENT OF CIVIC PARTICIPATION is the capacity for citizens to debate or deliberate about matters that are important to them and to come to consensus about the standards that govern them, formally and informally.[1] In religious communities, such deliberations often risk throwing people's foundational assumptions open to question. If foundational assumptions are those taken-for-granted understandings about what life is all about and what is simply essential, then deliberative processes of negotiation, consensus building, and competition can threaten to denaturalize people's most important organizing principles.[2] Members will be likely to attempt to rule certain debates as simply off-limits, even as others see those assumptions as precisely what needs to be renegotiated. If we want to understand *how* religious groups can shape civic participation, then, we must look to everyday interactions in which members define the terms and boundaries of legitimate social debate, as these terms and boundaries will govern what can result from members' deliberations.[3]

In what follows, I examine how church members defined "politics" in United Methodist debates about homosexuality as I observed them in the late 1990s, and I explore how these definitions set the limits of civic participation and the potential for social change. Religious organizations are not alone in using the category of politics to define the limits of acceptability; Nina Eliasoph (1998) observes a certain disdain for the category of politics in secular life, even in community organizations working for social change. Such distaste for politics can take on a special valence in religious communities because they are so often forums for explicitly discussing the essence of right and wrong.

In *God, Sex and Politics* (2004), I examined debates about homosexuality in two congregations; one was moving toward publicly affirming homosexuality, and the other maintained a more conservative stance of believing homosexuality to be sinful. I wanted to understand how people on different sides thought about homosexuality and how they came to know what they knew to be ultimately true, right, and good. In the course of discussions about homosexuality or other topics, I was struck as members on all sides expressed distaste when they invoked the category of politics—a category that could mean many different things but almost always meant something contrary to church members' vision of the Good, as opposed to the means to achieving that Good. This disdain for politics did not deter members from civic participation—far from it. By looking at what members said in distancing themselves from politics, we can see how the rhetoric of politics, as well as acts of avoiding the political altogether, worked to protect from negotiation people's foundational assumptions about what is ultimately unquestionable and true, their taken-for-granted assumptions that made life make sense to them.

After presenting a brief background, I discuss examples of religiously informed civic engagement in the form of two petitions, and I examine how antipolitical rhetoric worked to protect foundational assumptions from negotiation. By examining how members of the two congregations explicitly placed a value on avoiding conflict altogether, I then explore the other side of that desire to protect foundational assumptions. I conclude with some thoughts about what the tension between these two impulses might suggest for our analyses of American civic life and religion.

Background

On the issue of homosexuality over the last several decades, the United Methodist denomination has been contentiously split down the middle. Its stated policy, which members update every four years in a legislative conference, has maintained that homosexuality is contrary to Christian teaching.[4] The denomination forbids clergy from blessing or recognizing same-sex unions or allowing such ceremonies to take place in its buildings, and its policy at the time of my research was to deny ordination to those whom it called "self-avowed practicing homosexuals." At the same time, its doctrine states that sexuality is "God's good gift" to humanity and that all human beings are "of sacred worth"; such phrases and their ambiguities formed the basis for some members to challenge church policy (*Book of Discipline*, 1996, ¶304.3, ¶65G).[5]

To understand why debates about homosexuality were so explosive, I conducted participant observation and interviews in two congregations. I spent fourteen months observing the theologically more liberal one, which I call City Church. City Church had approximately one thousand members and was diverse economically and ethnically as well as theologically. Its leadership was theologically liberal, however, and pushed the congregation toward affirming homosexuality and publicly welcoming gay men and lesbians, sparking often-heated debates. I then spent seven months in the more conservative congregation, Missionary Church. About half the size of City Church, Missionary was economically similar to City Church but was almost entirely white and theologically conservative, and although a few members did privately confess to me that they did not think homosexuality was sinful, no one openly debated the church's teaching that indeed it was. In both congregations, I attended services, adult Sunday school classes, and Bible studies, as well as organizational and educational meetings where homosexuality or related issues were discussed. I also conducted unstructured, open-ended interviews with members to explore their thoughts about the issues. [6]

Among members of both congregations, views of homosexuality ranged, but all reflected more subtlety and moderation than we might think if we focus on media portrayals of the so-called culture wars.[7] At one end of the spectrum within these localities was the perspective that homosexuality is sinful, but that all human beings are sinners and should be welcome in the church. At the other end was the view that God made some people gay or lesbian, and that sex between two men or two women was therefore not inherently sinful.[8] Neither congregation fostered more "extreme" views, though members who disagreed with the predominant view in each congregation could feel beleaguered and silenced.

In both congregations, many members were civically engaged, participating in quiet pro-life or pro-choice demonstrations or walk-a-thons for AIDS service organizations and running food banks or other programs for homeless people. In both congregations, members could be found writing letters, signing petitions, and going to meetings to figure out how to effect change in the public sphere or the church. And in each, a handful of members engaged in denominational politics, organizing for or against the church affirming homosexuality, ordaining avowed gay men and lesbians, and blessing same-sex unions. In these cases, religious affiliation motivated civic participation and contributed to its meaningfulness. At the same time, I was struck by the extent to which members, even those engaged in these civic activities, distanced themselves from politics.

While civic life may offer spaces for citizens' deliberation, we should not assume that such spaces mirror the ideal public sphere, where individuals are equally free to raise their concerns and state their views.[9] In discussions of homosexuality, arguments that could not be made to fit certain unspoken formulas were, in effect, foreclosed—not necessarily because anyone intended to silence others, but because the communities were governed by an unspoken agreement about what church was *for*. While members may have agreed in principle that it was good to "be involved," love their neighbors, and witness against injustice, they defined this involvement against the specter of politics.

Petitions without Politics

That the category of politics meant something other than civic engagement is evident when we consider the example of two petitions—themselves acts of civic engagement—one of which explicitly cast politics in opposition to the Good. By examining the debates carried out through these petitions, we see how the very term "political" could serve to limit the legitimate scope of Christian thought and activity. In 1996, a group of pro-gay clergy circulated a petition titled "In All Things Charity" urging that the United Methodist Church change its policies regarding homosexuality.[10] The petition stated, "Scripture, tradition, reason and experience convince us that 'the practice of homosexuality' is not in itself 'incompatible with Christian teaching.'" Its signers saw the church's refusal to recognize and bless same-sex unions and ordain gay clergy as unconscionable. They stated, "We believe that public dissent from a teaching of the church must be done only prayerfully and with humility. However, we also believe that when we are confronted with an injustice, we must not remain silent." While they called their petition a "statement of conscience," these liberal clergy did not explicitly distance themselves from politics as they asserted that confronting injustice was their duty. "In All Things Charity" did not imply an opposition between politics and Christianity, but neither did it explicitly link the two.

A rebuttal titled "The More Excellent Way: God's Plan Re-Affirmed" was soon circulating. The statement explicitly accused the clergy who signed "In

All Things Charity" of neglecting Christian teaching and of being "politically motivated." It began:

> Although the authoritative witness of Scripture and Christian tradition teaches that the practice of homosexuality is a sin and that persons who practice such will not inherit the kingdom of God (cf. I Corinthians 6: 9-10), this witness has been diminished, ignored, and demeaned by individuals, groups and organizations within United Methodism who are committed to *a political agenda that is destructive to the nature and mission of the Church* and the moral fabric of society in general.

It concluded:

> We pray that the Church will move beyond this needless debate over an issue settled centuries ago and upheld throughout history by the unanimous witness of Scripture and Christian tradition. God's plan for humankind is not subject to modification according to the whims of personal experience or opinion. The Church will not abandon its biblical teachings on sin, repentance, forgiveness, salvation and sanctification in order to accommodate a culture at odds with the Gospel of Jesus Christ. Neither will the Church diminish its commitment to the sanctity of the marriage covenant and the integrity of the office of the ordained ministry in order to salve the consciences of a *politically motivated* constituency which knows not the radical demands of the life of holiness and discipleship. (emphases added)

Throughout the document and in no uncertain terms, the authors defined God's timeless "plan for humanity" in opposition to the "whims" of contemporary political motivations. "The More Excellent Way" explicitly tried to terminate the deliberation called for in the earlier statement; it defined the debate over homosexuality as "needless" and having been "settled centuries ago."

While positing Christianity, in opposition to politics, as the means to achieving the social good, the document's authors used the term *politics* to refer to supposedly fleeting concerns, borne out of contemporary secular life, while foreclosing the possibility that their own beliefs about sexuality and marriage were equally contemporary. This debate has been so explosive because participants have disagreed on the most fundamental question: What is timeless, sacred, and true? Both sides agreed that human society is not perfect, but they could not agree about what needed to change about it. Signers and supporters of "The More Excellent Way" saw scripture as clearly forbidding, in numerous passages, same-sex sexual behavior; to them, movements to accept homosexuality and equate it to heterosexuality seemed to stem from a culture predicated on sinful self-indulgence rather than righteous sacrifice.[11]

But these teachings did not seem timeless to the signers of "In All Things Charity" or to the supporters I heard from. Rather, such members posited their opponents' values as rooted either in the past or in contemporary human anxieties over sexuality. For the signers and supporters of "In All Things Charity," the scriptural passages that seemed to prohibit "homosexual practice" in fact condemned practices—such as temple prostitution and slave owners' sexual use of their slaves—that were common at the time the prohibitions were codified but in no way resembled today's loving, egalitarian, same-sex relationships.[12] They saw the Bible's truth inhering not in specific injunctions but in its overall message of loving God and one's neighbor. While supporters and signers of "The More Excellent Way" saw apparent biblical prohibitions on same-sex sexual activity as God's timeless truth, supporters and signers of "In All Things Charity" saw timelessness in what they described as God's universal love and justice.[13] Clearly, both sides held certain beliefs as foundational while they saw others' foundational assumptions as products of a particular earthly time and set of motivations.[14]

Protecting Church from Politics

In the congregations I examined, both conservative and pro-gay members echoed, in different ways, the authors' notion in "The More Excellent Way" that politics was opposite to church. Regardless of their views on homosexuality, many members of both congregations tended to distance themselves in one way or another from the category of politics by defining politics as the opposite of whatever they held as ideal—if the church ideal was selflessness, politics was selfish; if the ideal was faith, politics was based in fear; if the ideal was inclusion, politics was exclusive; if the ideal was unity, politics was division. In doing so, these members effectively protected their foundational assumptions from deliberation. If we see their ideals as sacred to members, we can say that politics was not simply "profane" but more akin to "evil"—a counterforce to the sacred with the unique power to threaten the sacred by threatening to reveal that it was not timeless truth but human construction

(Durkheim [1915] 1965; Berger 1969). Because of this tacit sense of evil, some members felt pressed to engage the debates on homosexuality precisely because they saw others as neglecting and threatening whatever they held as the essential, foundational Truth. This was the case in spite of a widespread and deep desire to keep church free from politics, conflict, and negotiation, to which we now turn.

A small portion of each congregation saw engagement over this issue as a crucial part of what they considered a Christian duty to witness to the world. At the same time, many members of the congregations I studied wanted to keep away from these national-level debates altogether. A number of members emphasized the danger these debates could pose to the church, precisely because such debates brought conflict into a realm that members wished to retain as a haven from conflict. Many saw political or social causes as fundamentally opposite to church. In this sense, members saw civic engagement as good if it meant helping those who needed help, but they saw the deliberative aspect of civic life as something that did not belong in church. By defining "human" deliberative processes as competitive and destructive, they implied that church should not be a place to talk through matters over which people were likely to disagree. In this context, the word *political* could come to mean simply "bad."

The notion that politics was bad seemed to shape what members could do and say while keeping their legitimacy in these congregations, especially in the more diverse City Church. One member elegantly expressed the antipathy toward politics that was implicit in others' remarks. In an adult Sunday school discussion, thirty-six-year-old Mindy Reynolds expressed a defense of the Promise Keepers, an evangelical men's organization, precisely because of what she saw as their nonpolitical goals. When the Promise Keepers hosted a large gathering in Washington, D.C., in 1997, Mindy explained that she saw their goal as holding men accountable to God and to their own families. She expressed her exasperation with feminist protests of the event, saying,

The Promise Keepers are wanting to get men together in Washington, and I don't see why those women are protesting them. I think it's really exciting. Not everything has to be political. Why do they have to call it political? If women can get together and no one complains, why shouldn't the men? If they're going to go back to their families and help with the kids instead of working so much, then that's good. If you're just doing something, and I attribute something bad to your actions, that's just my bad thinking. If the Promise Keepers are getting together, and the women want to say that they're being political, that's because *the women* are the ones being political.

Regardless of how we might agree or disagree with Mindy's remarks, what is striking here is the extent to which Mindy saw politics as "something bad" and "bad thinking." When feminist organizations criticized the Promise Keepers, they saw themselves as defending feminist gains, including increased equality in the workplace as well as within heterosexual couples; the Promise Keepers' goal, on the other hand, was to help men take back what they taught was men's rightful duty to lead their families. The controversy was over which grounding assumptions should be taken for granted as natural: hierarchical gender roles or the fundamental equality of individuals. But this debate was beside the point for Mindy. In her remarks, the question about which group was political seems to have amounted to a question about which had the better intentions—the group that wanted to help men and their families, or the group that criticized them.

Few members went so far as to call politics "bad thinking," though many saw political or social causes as fundamentally opposite to church. For instance, Missionary Church member Al Delacroix, a computer programmer in his fifties, took issue with the United Methodist Church for what he saw as its overeagerness to adopt social causes. He commented on the "turmoil" he saw Methodists creating in trying to address controversial social issues, remarking,

> I've had a problem with the Methodist church for a long time. It's involved itself with social issues on way too many occasions. One of the things that I like about the Baptist church when I was going there was that as children were growing up, they were being taught the Bible. Not social issues. [When] we got out of the Baptist church we began to get into social issues. Well, I got out of the Baptist church right around 1960, and well, you can imagine what kind of turmoil we went through in the next decade, because we went through Vietnam, we went through the Civil Rights Act, we came through so many different things that our church was just constantly in turmoil over, you know, "What should we be doing? What should we be doing?" Basically, my feeling is if you're a church, you should concern yourself with Christian doctrine and the Bible. Period. That's it. Why get all tied up in all that other crap? Okay, that's a non-missionary attitude, but it's the way I feel.

In the last sentence of this excerpt, Al seems to have recognized that many church members might have seen it as Christian duty to reach out to people in crisis and help, perhaps, to deliberate and discern answers. But, he said, he felt that such "crap" distracted people from more important things. In effect, he seems to have seen negotiation about the social world, and the conflicts that can follow from these negotiations, as the opposite of what church is for.

Unlike most of his fellow Missionary Church members, Al did not believe homosexuality to be sinful, so I asked what he thought about his denomination's ban on ordaining "self-avowed practicing homosexuals." He replied,

> I got no problem with that. If somebody wants to be a minister, and they want to be a homosexual, okay, go somewhere else. Every day I get up and I drive to work and there's a speed limit. . . . If I choose to go eighty miles an hour, I'm gonna get a ticket. . . . I'm gonna obey it or I'm gonna pay the price. And if you decide that you want to be a homosexual, and you know that the Methodist Church has got these rules that say we absolutely will not [condone that], then go somewhere else. The word of God is not just Methodist, it's a lot of other things.

When I asked where they should go, he remarked,

> Well, they may even have to start their own church. The homosexual movement would not be the first group to start one; Methodism was an offshoot [of the Episcopal Church]. If you can't work within the group, get out of the group and start your own group. . . . It's just common sense. But why go in and just try to make it a battle all the time? What's the point of that? All that does is make you draw lines in the sand and choose sides. That's not what the Christian faith is supposed to be about.

Al equated working for change with picking fights and choosing sides, while he saw Christianity as ideally about unity in faith. In his view, God is capacious enough to include many views, not just the Methodists', but people themselves might need to separate in order to focus on God rather than fight with each other. His desire to avoid conflict protects a number of things from questioning; it protects the local status quo, but it also protects his own notion of Christianity's central premises and what those premises mean. So long as those who disagree respond solely by flight, he seemed to say, no one's views need be challenged, and they need not be distracted from their faith.

Others might embrace the social issues Al saw as so distracting, but they too could see conflict and negotiation as the opposite of what church was supposed to be about. Keith Appleton was a thirtyish computer programmer at City Church. When I asked him whether he felt City Church should bless same-sex unions, he replied,

> Yeah, they should. But they can't right now. It would tear the church apart. . . . It would be a national controversy. To get into that debate would put me in the place of people being mean, and I don't like that. I don't want to be there.
>
> People on each side try to punish each other; each side sees it as *we* have to win and *they* have to lose. They can't just sit down over dinner and argue about it. It's too important to each side to win or destroy the other side. And they *should* be discussing it. Christians should be discussing it because it gets to the very heart about what they believe about relationships and society. (reconstructed from notes)

For Keith, even if the church should ideally be a forum for deliberation, he did not want his *own* congregation to be that forum. To him, such debate would position members to try to destroy each other, introducing conflict where he did not want it.

Keith's remarks suggest that he thought the church would be the ideal site for civic deliberation, except that people's imperfections would lead them to escalate disagreements, be mean, and tear the church apart. In effect, he lacked faith that the church could be a site for civil—in both senses of the term—debate. Forty-five-year-old Ruthie Shafer echoed Keith's understanding of the conflict between the deliberative ideal and human weakness. Thinking about debates in City Church, she explained,

> To the extent that we come together, and spend time together, and we learn from each other, in formal and informal ways, then we will evolve as a community. And so, you and I have differing opinions, and our opinions will be modified and our approach will be different. That's the healthy way to do it. The polarized way of doing things, in *human* methodology, at the other end of the line, is you and I have a disagreement and it escalates and escalates and we become polarized not just because of our ideas but now because you're pushing me. So now I must become positioned with my ideal because it's my weapon, and the ultimate of that is war. So as Christians we've been given, if you will, tools for working with each other and caring for each other, but we fall short in using them.

For Ruthie, the "human," more earthly way was one of polarization and war, while the Godly ideal was of love and learning. Repeatedly, members in both congregations on both sides of the homosexuality debate phrased their religious ideals in terms of creating cohesion rather than division and destruction. Numerous members decried any sort of contest requiring the production of winners and losers, and they saw the Christian ideal as creating a situation where no one should have to lose.

A tension emerges, in that like the authors of the petitions, Ruthie did hold certain ideals as sacred and unquestionable. And she saw their opposite as politics. Thinking about those she saw as unwelcoming to gay men and lesbians in the congregation, she remarked,

> But, see, I believe that all of us who exclude others from the faith are messing with "the Man," as they say. That is a big no-no. That is a big, big, big, no-no. Scripture says be very, very, very concerned if you are a person who helps to move one of these little ones away from God. I mean, there is some very strong imagery in that. So anyone who is involved, I think, in making people feel uncomfortable, even if it's as simple as someone whom you know to be gay walks into the church with their partner and you turn your head, and you don't welcome them, I believe that you will be accountable for that. Yes I do. And if you have formed [anti-gay] collectives where that's your mission, and you are part of that set of politics—oh, I don't want to be around, it's not going to be any fun. I don't know what all the penalties are, but I know that there's a current life penalty for that kind of mindset; it's a kind of living death that people can experience when they are in that, uh, that politic.

Ruthie considered inclusion so sacred that she could cast those "political" figures—those who did not welcome gay men and lesbians—as the "living dead," secure in her faith that they would have to answer to God. From her earlier remarks, she seems to have held a particular ideal for deliberation: "In formal and informal ways," those who disagree over homosexuality should be able to show each other care and evolve as a community. But at the same time, she posited that those who see homosexuality as sinful should somehow come to shed their own foundational assumptions and realize that the church is for everyone, so gays should be truly welcome.

Like the signers and supporters of "The More Excellent Way," Ruthie's foundational assumptions were just that: *foundational* to her faith and worldview.

Debates about homosexuality are so explosive, in fact, because they threaten to reveal church members' very different understandings of God and humanity and expose them to denaturalizing deliberation. These debates were thus shaped by members' competing attempts to shield their own foundational assumptions from such threats. In any given debate, the terrain will be shaped by who, if anyone, the community accords the authority to define which assumptions will be treated as Godly or natural and which will be treated as human error.[15]

Communicative Rationality in Church

If we are interested in the role organized religion plays in civic life, we must pay careful attention to how members define their ideals, how they see those ideals relating to processes of deliberation, and given those worldviews, what they *do*. Religious convictions compelled some members to mobilize and engage in collective action to improve society and the church. At the same time, we have seen members suggesting that politics is illegitimate because it involves questioning things that some members did not believe should be negotiated. If members of a religious group accept the definition of *politics* as worldly and divisive and *religion* as otherworldly and communitarian, politics itself can seem contrary to religious life. And as the competing petitions demonstrate, casting an argument as "politically motivated" can delegitimate it if people define politics as opposite to proper religious motivations, especially in the absence of a counterargument. If politics is defined as that which simply questions the "wrong" truths, then legitimate civic participation is severely limited in what it can open to negotiation, and negotiations will take an explosive tone.

Analyzing two national petitions, I have shown how the term *politics* forecloses negotiation of certain assumptions that the authors and signers wish to take for granted as essentially true. Considering the strong antipathy I observed in the two congregations toward whatever members called "political," it becomes clear that we need to track the work such words do when we see them used: To what are they opposed, and what do they foreclose? Asking these questions allows us to see what assumptions help members define the community of debate, as well as how these assumptions limit and direct those debates.

We have also seen from our observation of members of these two congregations that a tension exists between feeling a duty to defend one's foundational assumptions and a profound desire to preserve them from questioning in the first place (Berger 1969; Fish 1997). Members such as Mindy, Al, Keith, and Ruthie made clear that they saw deliberation itself as distancing people from God and God's ways, distracting them from what church was supposed to be for. Their comments suggest that they saw politics or deliberation embroiling people in battles instead of helping them do what they thought members should be doing—discerning God's will and sharing God's love.

Even those members who actively participated in the deliberations could express frustration at the deliberative process. One City Church member, thirty-five-year-old Linda Renaldi, favored making church policy more gay-affirming and organized meetings to discuss this issue. Even so, she remarked,

> I guess what we're all hoping is that [the congregation's Administrative Council] will vote yes [to affirming homosexuality], and then we'll just deal with the fallout; I mean, that's what I'm hoping. [We're] just trying to get it done, and move into the positive phase of it. I don't know, I guess me coordinating those meetings was my contribution to it, but I'm *over* it. I have a major chip on my shoulder with people who don't get it by now. I'm like, "Hello! Wake up! It's not your job to judge who gets in and who doesn't. So just shut up, or get out." That's kind of where I am right now. Which is not the best attitude to have. Obviously . . . I just have trouble getting past the audacity.

Linda found it aggravatingly "audacious" for other church members to assert that homosexuality was not part of God's plan or was incompatible with Christian teaching, and like the others, she was frustrated that the debates had persisted for as long as they had. She was ready for the deliberations to cease, as they elicited hostility that she did not want to experience.

Yet we must not allow members' desire for a haven from politics to lead us to believe that religiously sponsored deliberations on social issues cannot be a form of civic engagement. Religious groups are important to the civic sphere. By organizing to discuss some less threatening and less foundation-shattering questions than homosexuality, religious groups help to create a social infrastructure that can, at times, allow their members to take on deeper social questions in a climate of more trust and respect. I was humbled early on in my fieldwork to witness the amount of work and thought that members of these small communities put into negotiating with each other and by the extent to which they dealt with each other as fellow human beings rather than as stereotypes. They might have been angry at each other, but many of them tried to understand where others were coming from and tried to find a common language to change each other's minds; occasionally they were open to changing their own. Even as Linda privately expressed to me the anger she felt toward those members who disagreed with her about the church's policies, she could appreciate their capacity to grow and change. Thinking about a member who was vocal in his belief that homosexuality was sinful, she reflected,

> He is great. He's made a major turnaround. Before, he was like, "It's a sin. Die in Hell!" And now he's just kind of—okay, he thinks about it. And he's trying to learn and evolve, and I think it's really *cool*. And I think they really care about City Church. I know everybody does. Everyone cares about their walk with their God, and they care about the church, and I know everyone is as passionate in their beliefs and as sincere about it as I am.

Linda's colorfully hyperbolic comments do not necessarily tell us much about what her fellow church member actually thought or said, but they may tell us about her own evolution. For just as she saw him as having once condemned gay men and lesbians, she relates to us her own transformation from once having seen him in such hostile, stark terms to seeing him as a fellow member struggling to make sense of life, to discern God's will, and to do what's right.[16]

In every sense of the term, congregations can be forums for civil exchange. As we think about this kind of civility, though, we should always look for what assumptions are taken for granted to allow that kind of civility to take place and what those particular assumptions foreclose.

Notes

1. I use the term *citizen* in its broader sense to refer to those who belong to a polity regardless of formal citizenship status.

2. In Berger's (1969) terms, these foundational assumptions help to form the *nomos*, or meaningful world order. Deliberation over these assumptions can thus threaten to introduce anomie. For more on congregational conflicts, see Ammerman (1997), Becker (1999), and Becker and Eiesland (1997).

3. Distinguishing between "civic" and "political" processes, Paul Lichterman (2005) calls for us to attend to the processes by which religious groups define their

civic work as "political" or "not political," and this chapter can be seen as an answer to that call.

4. See Wood and Bloch (1995).

5. The 1996 edition of the *Book of Discipline* was current during my research. While the wording and organization have changed slightly in subsequent revisions, the policies have not dramatically changed as of this printing.

6. Quotations from respondents all come from tape-recorded and transcribed interviews, unless otherwise noted.

7. The term comes from Hunter (1991); for critiques see, for instance, Williams (1997).

8. "Gay men and lesbians" or "homosexuals" were generally the terms of discussion; bisexuals and transgendered people were rarely included in the discussions.

9. Habermas (1991); for critiques of this view, see Calhoun (1992).

10. Both "In All Things Charity" and the rebuttal "The More Excellent Way" are reprinted in *Transforming Congregations* (1997).

11. Biblical passages cited to make this case include: Genesis 19:1–29; Leviticus 18:19–23, 20:13; I Corinthians 6:9–11; Romans 1:26–27; and I Timothy 1:8–11.

12. For examples of pro-gay Protestant theology and history, see Boswell (1980, 1994), Countryman (1988), Heyward (1984, 1989), Horner (1978), Scanzoni and Mollenkott (1994), and Scroggs (1983).

13. For brief arguments from both sides, see Geis and Messer (1994). For more scholarly approaches to debates over homosexuality across religions, see Olyan and Nussbaum (1998) and Swidler (1993).

14. In reality, there were more than two sets of opinions expressed in these debates. A number of members, for instance, agreed that the church's role was to love and welcome everybody, even as it maintained that same-sex sexual love was not in God's plan. Some (including, no doubt, many signers of "The More Excellent Way") supported "ex-gay" movements, which try to help gays put what they see as the sin of homosexuality behind them (see Erzen 2006; Moon 2005a; Wolkomir 2006). Others favored less discussion and debate on the matter, thinking that people should "mind their own business." When it came to matters of church policy, however, these debates often boiled down to yes or no questions, such as whether or not homosexuality could be compatible with Christian teachings. These debates had a polarizing effect reflected in this yes or no question.

15. See Moon (2005a, 2005b) for deeper explorations of how unspoken assumptions about heterosexuality shaped the outcomes of these debates.

16. In this sense, congregations can be sites for political engagement in the form of what Habermas called communicative rationality—discussion whose goal is mutual understanding rather than winning against an opponent, as Michele

Dillon (1999) points out. Dillon posits Foucault's and Habermas's approaches to power in late-modernity as incommensurable, though this case suggests that discursive power can be at work even as participants in a debate decry the kinds of instrumental (combative, competitive) rationality Habermas sees as colonizing all aspects of life. Although it is beyond the scope of this chapter, synthesizing these two approaches to power might provide a useful way to consider the power at work in everyday life.

Works Cited

Ammerman, Nancy Tatom. 1997. *Congregation and Community*. New Brunswick, NJ: Rutgers University Press.

Becker, Penny Edgell. 1999. *Congregations in Conflict: Cultural Models of Local Religious Life*. New York: Cambridge University Press.

Becker, Penny Edgell, and Nancy L. Eiesland, eds. 1997. *Contemporary American Religion: An Ethnographic Reader*. Walnut Creek, CA: AltaMira Press.

Berger, Peter L. 1969. *The Sacred Canopy: Elements of a Sociological Theory of Religion*. New York: Anchor.

Book of Discipline of the United Methodist Church. 1996. Nashville, TN: The United Methodist Publishing House.

Boswell, John. 1980. *Christianity, Social Tolerance and Homosexuality: Gay People in Western Europe from the Beginning of the Christian Era to the Fourteenth Century*. Chicago: University of Chicago Press.

———. 1994. *Same-Sex Unions in Premodern Europe*. New York: Random House.

Calhoun, Craig, ed. 1992. *Habermas and the Public Sphere*. Cambridge, MA: MIT Press.

Countryman, William. 1988. *Dirt, Greed, and Sex: Sexual Ethics in the New Testament and Their Implications for Today*. Philadelphia: Fortress Press.

Dillon, Michele. 1999. *Catholic Identity: Balancing Reason, Faith and Power*. New York: Cambridge University Press.

Durkheim, Emile. [1915] 1965. *The Elementary Forms of the Religious Life*. New York: The Free Press.

Eliasoph, Nina. 1998. *Avoiding Politics: How Americans Produce Apathy in Everyday Life*. New York: Cambridge University Press.

Erzen, Tanya. 2006. *Straight to Jesus: Sexual and Christian Conversions in the Ex-Gay Movement*. Berkeley: University of California Press.

Fish, Stanley. 1997. "Boutique Multiculturalism, or Why Liberals Are Incapable of Thinking about Hate Speech." *Critical Inquiry* 23:378–95.

Geis, Sally B., and Donald E. Messer, eds. 1994. *Caught in the Crossfire: Helping Christians Debate Homosexuality*. Nashville, TN: Abingdon Press.

Habermas, Jürgen. 1984. *The Theory of Communicative Action*. Boston: Beacon Press.

———. 1991. *The Structural Transformation of the Public Sphere: An Inquiry into a Category of Bourgeois Society.* Cambridge, MA: MIT Press.

Heyward, Carter. 1984. *Our Passion for Justice: Images of Power, Sexuality, and Liberation.* Cleveland, OH: Pilgrim Press.

———. 1989. *Touching Our Strength: The Erotic as Power and the Love of God.* New York: HarperCollins.

Horner, Tom. 1978. *Jonathan Loved David: Homosexuality in Biblical Times.* Philadelphia: Westminster Press.

Hunter, James Davison. 1991. *Culture Wars: The Struggle to Define America.* New York: Basic Books.

Lichterman, Paul. 2005. *Elusive Togetherness: Church Groups Trying to Bridge America's Divisions.* Princeton, NJ: Princeton University Press.

Moon, Dawne. 2004. *God, Sex and Politics: Homosexuality and Everyday Theologies.* Chicago: University of Chicago Press.

———. 2005a. "Discourse, Interaction, and the Making of Selves in the US Protestant Dispute over Homosexuality." *Theory and Society* 34:551–77.

———. 2005b. "Emotion Language and Social Power: Homosexuality and Narratives of Pain in Church." *Qualitative Sociology* 28, no. 4:325–47.

Olyan, Saul M., and Martha C. Nussbaum. 1998. *Sexual Orientation and Human Rights in American Religious Discourse.* New York: Oxford University Press.

Scanzoni, Letha, and Virginia Ramsey Mollenkott. 1994. *Is the Homosexual My Neighbor? A Positive Christian Response.* San Francisco: Harper.

Scroggs, Robin. 1983. *The New Testament and Homosexuality: Contextual Background for Contemporary Debate.* Philadelphia: Fortress Press.

Swidler, Arlene, ed. 1993. *Homosexuality and World Religions.* Harrisburg, PA: Trinity Press International.

Transforming Congregations, newsletter. 1997. Bakersfield, CA, April–June.

Williams, Rhys H. 1997. *Cultural Wars in American Politics: Critical Reviews of a Popular Myth.* New York: Aldine de Gruyter.

Wolkomir, Michelle. 2006. *Be Not Deceived: The Sacred and Sexual Struggles of Gay and Ex-Gay Christian Men.* New Brunswick, NJ: Rutgers University Press.

Wood, James R., and Jon P. Bloch. 1995. "The Role of Church Assemblies in Building a Civil Society: The Case of the United Methodist General Conference's Debate on Homosexuality." *Sociology of Religion* 56, no. 2:121–36.

8   Conclusion: Rethinking Religion's Civic Life
Paul Lichterman and C. Brady Potts

OUR OPENING CHAPTER INTRODUCED OPTIMISTIC AND pessimistic perspectives on the civic life of religion. The pessimistic outlook tends to assume that when religion goes public, it turns the civic arena into a zone of competition, perhaps even a battlefield. The optimistic outlook sees religious organizations as a vital part of American civic life with a distinguished history. Participating in what we have called a "Tocquevillian celebration," optimists invoke a particular reading of Alexis de Tocqueville. Tocqueville proposed in *Democracy in America* that American religion would be a source of trust and moral stability for a democratic, highly individualistic society. Tocqueville's overall portrait of America's civic possibilities was more ambivalent and complicated, though. His assessment of religion's contributions was more nuanced than some optimists' very straightforward claims would have it. "Tocquevillian celebration" describes the currently popular but more partial reading of Tocqueville that leads religion's civic boosters to hope that church congregations, interfaith organizations, or religiously based social services will cultivate social connections and generate a sense of communal obligation toward the public at large. This Tocquevillian celebration hopes that religious groups can restore an ailing and increasingly fragmented society.

Looking back at the research presented by our contributors, one first impression would be that the optimists are off the mark. The civic "promise" of religious associations does not seem to meet the great expectations of Tocquevillian celebrants. Religious associations sponsor a significant amount of volunteering in the United States, but we learn that these associations' contributions to public life, including political and social service activity, are smaller than some would hope. Religious organizations contribute more to the sphere of artistic endeavors in the United States than they do to civic and political or social service relationships. Further, although religious organizations make up a plurality of voluntary associational memberships in the United States, the connections people forge as fellow congregation members are not simply interchangeable with other kinds of relations in civic life.[1] Optimists might hope that religious congregations spiral ties outward in all directions. We find instead that their ideas of "community" are not all-encompassing but are bounded and variable. Optimists might hope that religious associations, like any other associations, would host thoughtful, wide-ranging deliberation on issues of public concern—discussions that renew feelings and ideas and enlarge the heart, to invoke Tocqueville's famous metaphors. We find instead that deliberation in religious associations may not live up to this ideal of the public sphere.[2]

The overviews and cases presented in this volume would frustrate pessimists too, though they may appear to be closer to the mark—at least initially. On the one hand, the groups in our authors' studies produced quite limited versions of the civic goods that optimists would hope religiously based civic engagement generates. Nevertheless, the pessimist take on religion in public fails to describe what actually transpired in these groups and cannot account for the reasons why the aggregate of congregations and civic organizations described or summarized in this volume failed to live up to the highest hopes of religion's civic boosters. Little in the preceding chapters would suggest strongly that membership in religious associations was a means to greater social status beyond those associations or that theologically driven, "warring" words or ideas wracked local civic life. What dilemmas or disappointments members faced did not always derive directly from religious beliefs. When religion ended up dividing people, as Omar McRoberts found while observing church-neighborhood relations in a Boston religious district, it was not caused by the polarization between religious "reds" and "blues" that popular journalism likes to see in the American public. And while the group contexts explored in Paul Lichterman's and Dawne Moon's studies did set distinctive limits on communication among the members, it was not the case that religious and civic speech were incompatible. Their groups did provide a forum for public discussions that are relatively hard to find elsewhere.

The Tocquevillian celebration has depended on simple, normative definitions of religion as a moral stabilizer and civic groups as generators of citizenly discourse and broad solidarity. We appreciate Michael Schudson's alternative perspective that different historical periods with different institutional arrangements have cultivated different definitions of civic virtue. Borrowing the logic of his perspective, we could say that to expect voluntary citizen groups, religious or otherwise, to generate enduring social ties and deeply critical deliberation may be to force civic ideals of a different age onto our own. Why should we be surprised that church groups offer relatively little social service when social service has been professionalized in the United States for decades? Schudson observes too that civic engagement is increasingly individualistic, event-centered, and correspondingly less likely to transpire in the types of enduring, face-to-face volunteer organizations that Tocqueville lauded and that Robert Putnam and Theda Skocpol favor in the same spirit. On that view, it would not necessarily impugn the civic virtue of congregations to observe, as Nancy Ammerman does, that they respond to local crises—race riots in Rodney King's Los Angeles of 1992 to give an example—even if they don't always produce enduring civic coalitions. And in a society that prizes individual expression and individual rights and builds them into the fabric of its institutions, it is not surprising that American religion increasingly is personalized and self-chosen, and that deliberations on homosexuality in congregations are constrained by a hesitance to offend feelings.

In all, overoptimistic understandings of civic life are historically myopic; worse, they won't help us understand empirically why some religious congregations and groups may not meet optimistic expectations while others might in some ways. By assuming that civic groups and religion both are generally good for society, Tocquevillian optimists risk treating both as essences instead of (variable) relationships and practices. This turns our attention away from processes that may make religious groups frustrate many observers' expectations, whether optimistic or pessimistic.

It takes more than several local cases and a couple of overview statements to assess definitively the civic life of religion in America. But the material in this volume is enough for us to propose a new orienting perspective for additional research. We find that Schudson's historically informed sensibilities are more realistic than those of the optimistic, received Tocqueville—someone Tocqueville himself might recognize only dimly—of some contemporary research.[3] In that spirit, and in light of this volume's findings, we take the next step and propose a more realistic starting point for understanding religious associations' civic contributions.

Religiously based voluntary associations are in many ways like any of the other kinds of voluntary associations in the United States. They are subject to the same kinds of forces—in terms of social organization and cultural and material constraints—as similar groups that may undertake civic projects in the United States. They need to maintain themselves as organizations, recruit and hold on to members, and establish a common world for members to inhabit in the course of being involved with the group, all with the resources available to them. It is not the case that these associations' religious (rather than secular) bases simply diminish their ability to produce the public goods theorists have expected of vigorous civic engagement. Their religious bases give them some *distinctive* limits and potential as sites of civic life, but we need not think of these conditions as fundamentally more formidable, rich, or ennobling. Finally, alongside a more manifold understanding of religious associations' civic potential and drawbacks, we benefit from understanding religion as a product of interactions and institutions rather than as an essential belief system that drives people to act.

Rather than accept optimists' or pessimists' a priori evaluations, scholars need to look and listen more closely to what religious organizations actually do in civic life. Research needs to pay attention to the institutional arrangements that make religious organizations' civic activities possible. In light of this perspective, we revisit our contributors' arguments and cases and suggest specific directions for future research on the civic life of religion.

Sacred Groups and Mundane Realities: Beyond the Tocquevillian Celebration

Both Nancy Ammerman and Mark Chaves show that many, if not most, of a typical congregation's activities are devoted to internal organizational matters and specifically religious practices rather than to "reaching out" across social distances and forging connections that can bridge a diverse society. In the context of some policymakers' high hopes that religious associations can address society's problems, it is worth hearing Ammerman and Chaves's reminder that congregations above all are religious entities and devote their energies accordingly. As Ammerman might put it, to know a congregation's potential for building civic bridges outward, we need to know first how the congregation constitutes itself as a religious collectivity.

This may seem like a failing to those who value purely civic ends. Yet it helps to remember that most organizations expend a great deal of energy in legitimating themselves and in demonstrating that they are what they say they are. For a congregation to undertake a set of social service tasks, it must first do all the things that make it a congregation and not a social service agency or voters' league.[4] The same applies to any formal organization. The members of Rotary Clubs and fraternal orders, to cite two archetypical forms of American civic organization, reach out to their local social worlds, but they also spend a great deal of time on organizational rituals—meeting, banqueting, inducting new members.[5] Though the Tocquevillian celebration seems off cue when it comes to religious groups' bridge-building, it does not follow that these groups are inherently more insular simply because they are religious groups.

Omar McRoberts shows how both internal symbolism and external organizational forces shape a church's relationship to the neighborhood in which it is located. In the case of his Boston churches, local geopolitical constraints as well as religiously based symbolic boundaries often work at cross-purposes with local civic engagement. The majority of the churches in his study understood the "street" as a profane and even evil place, so church-goers in the religious district largely avoided broader neighborhood ties in favor of fellowship with other congregants. The networks these churches generated related only very thinly to the neighborhoods that make up the religious district.

Yet creating and maintaining symbolic boundaries is a central feature of most group life; congregations and religious associations are hardly distinctive in that way.[6] Symbolic boundaries help groups make sense of the world in both secular and religious settings. The separation between the church and the street in the world of urban religious districts is not so fundamentally different from moral boundaries drawn on the basis of class, or of distinctions between public and private that organize political action.[7]

We need to assess religious associations' capacity for democratic deliberation as well as bridge-building more realistically. Recall that in the Tocquevillian vision, citizens discuss public issues, determine the common good, and slowly learn to understand fellow citizens who may be quite different from themselves. In their chapters, both Lichterman and Moon find that religious settings constrain deliberation in particular and often unexpected ways.

Lichterman finds that certain kinds of religious personhood, such as the "servant," proscribe deliberation altogether, while others may allow participants to express righteous anger in biblical terms once in a while, but only with the understanding that biblically based *deliberation* is not what a decent religious person does most of the time. The latter case is especially significant since many Americans would consider religious idioms and language powerful symbolic forces in American public life, and at least some social scientists agree with them. Maybe ironically, popular understandings of religious identity put a damper on explicit religious reasoning in local civic settings beyond the media spotlight. This reticence about voicing religious reasons is quite different from commonsense understandings of public religion we would gather from watching conservative Christian spokespeople on television. Images of Bible-thumping certainty, Lichterman suggests, are part of what makes some church-going civic group members wary of religious talk in their groups at all.

Moon's study of debates over homosexuality in theologically liberal and conservative congregations brings to light a distancing from "politics" that other researchers have recently observed. Moon shows that in these settings the avoidance of political debate serves to protect deeply held foundational assumptions. Participants in church discussions on the hot-button issue of homosexuality avoided debate that otherwise threatened to denaturalize foundational religious beliefs. Discussion in such settings may expand hearts and minds, but it proceeds only along lines that preserve deeply held religious understandings about the world. Those lines are not the same as the ones associated with "culture wars" between liberals and conservatives.

Culture and group dynamics may keep religious congregations and associations from being sites of sustained deliberation, yet, deliberation is difficult for many kinds of voluntary associations; again, religious groups are hardly distinctive here. If religious culture constrains deliberation in these settings, so do other cultural formations structure interaction in secular group settings.[8] Groups fail to create spaces for truly critical deliberation for many reasons. A group's "political etiquette" may, for instance, hold that critical discussion constitutes "getting on a high horse." Or group members may assume that deliberation about public issues is a waste of time when there are tasks to carry out and needy people to help. For many Americans, talk is "mere talk"; talk does not accomplish much.[9] Religion, in short, does not corner the market on political avoidance in the United States. Thus, we should study the institutional, organizational, or cultural conditions that make critical deliberation more or less possible within religious associations.[10]

Finally, just as the secular processes of urbanization and racial segregation intrude on the symbolic life of religious districts, as McRoberts shows, so too do secular vocabularies, discourses, and symbolic orders crop up in everyday religious settings. The language of emotion that Moon's churchgoers employed in their deliberation over the issue of homosexuality, for example, is one that should be familiar to observers of American culture.[11] It is therefore doubly dangerous to reduce the culture of religious organizations to formal or theological elements. Just as there may be customary religious knowledge that has little to do with any "official" texts, secular culture also powerfully shapes religious organizations. This may be explicit, as when congregations adopt secular organizational models (i.e., committees or boards, rather than elders or deacons) or import popular music styles into "modern" worship services in an effort to retain younger members. Or it may happen in ways that members may take for granted, as when pastors or congregants rely on widely shared, often mass-mediated frames to interpret current events in their sermons or social outreach committees. Religious culture is not the only kind of culture that matters in religious associations. Let's expand on this large, potentially counterintuitive point.

Avoiding an Essentialism of Religious Beliefs

Celebrants of religion's social virtues, detractors of religion, and many people in general share a commonsense theological determinism. They assume that public religious groups are groups that are propelled *directly* by religious beliefs. On this view, such groups are doing what they think "God says" one should do in a given situation. The essays in this volume have shown that this beliefs-centered understanding of religious groups, while certainly not entirely wrong, glosses over a variety of phenomena at the organizational, situational, and broader cultural levels that shape the civic life of religious groups—*that help constitute the practice of religion.* Even the most other-worldly strains of religion are, sociologically speaking, embedded in a world of cultural understandings, preferred ways of speaking, and routine styles of acting that do not derive directly from sacred texts and that set limits on what it is possible to say, do, think, or be. From a social science point of view, theological beliefs and practices don't exist except as embedded in cultural contexts. Rather than assume the perspective of groups who see themselves as fundamentally set apart from the cultural world by their religious nature, sociological analysis must keep the socially, culturally embedded character of religious groups in mind when investigating how they become civically engaged.[12]

If we limit our questions about culture and communication in religious groups to questions about what those groups' religious beliefs make them say or do, then we miss learning about the different ways people relate to religious beliefs. We miss other forms of culture, not directly or obviously religious, that influence them too, or else we assume these are part of the group's "belief system," available somewhere in the sacred texts motivating the group. If we rely on the notion that religious beliefs must be by far the main ideas that matter in religious groups, then we figure a group's ideas about civic engagement must come pretty directly from its theology. We assume that knowing a group's official religious beliefs tells us just about all that is interesting to know about the group *as* a religious group. Proceeding this way, we would be courting an essentialism of religious beliefs.

Of course, sociologists of religion have long observed that religious collectivities take form in a broader cultural context. Decades ago Peter Berger and Thomas Luckmann remarked that consumerism drove Americans to choose congregations the way shoppers look for the best package deal. More recently sociologists have focused on the widespread organizational forms that suffuse the American religious world as much as other spheres, making some aspects of congregational life very much like a bureaucracy or a therapy group.[13] Religious people live in sociocultural milieus that are not simply "add-ons" or optional aspects of lives already religious but embody religious lives and constitute religious collectivities. This basic sociological insight is crucial if we want to understand the civic life of religion.

In short, there is more continuity than disconnect between religious and secular voluntary organizations in terms of their group-level processes and their civic potential. They maintain boundaries between themselves and other groups. They have relationships with their surroundings that do not derive exclusively from their theologies or from religious vocabularies.

The Next Questions

This volume suggests new starting points for studying and discussing religion's civic life. We read the chapters as a collective invitation to drop much of the strongly normative definition of civic life as a sphere of self-sacrificing, ever-expanding regard for the public good. The contributors invite us to consider the possibility that religious associations produce the goods of public deliberation or bridge-building unpredictably. And they ask us to remember that the civic life of religion depends on more than the power or distinctiveness of religious culture; it depends substantially on organizational and larger cultural realities that help to structure the internal life of religious associations and the external opportunities associations find for civic engagement. While we have considered only U.S. cases, we find these to be sound starting points for discussions of the civic life of religion around the globe. What would they mean concretely for research? We conclude by posing several research questions, which move from the broadest institutional level to the local, everyday settings of civic life.

How Do Different Regimes of Religious Participation Open or Close Opportunities for Religious Citizenship?

Religion scholars regularly observe that religious disestablishment in the United States conditions the possibilities for religious participation in American civic life, directly and indirectly. Since religious disestablishment makes congregational participation a voluntary choice in a "free market," congregations must work at attracting and maintaining members, which in turn conditions the ways they will conceive civic projects. Constitutional law permits, conditions, or proscribes religious participation in civic life in many nations. Constitutional law is a backbone for a set of social arrangements, which we will call "regimes" of religious participation—institutionalized expectations about the role of religion or religious identities in public. Comparing religious associations in different nations in light of different constitutional frameworks, we can avoid mistakenly attributing differences between nations purely to religious differences or national or local cultural traditions. When constitutional arrangements change, as in post-Soviet Russia or post-revolutionary Iran, for instance, we might expect obvious changes in a society's regime of religious participation even as some of the society's cultural and religious traditions endure.

New national legislation as well as slower, subtler cultural changes also may or may not generate new regimes of religious participation. The 1996 welfare policy reforms in the United States and changes in European social provision roughly around the same time are producing new expectations or conflicting expectations regarding the proper civic role of religious associations.

There are many good empirical questions to ask about how, and how much, these changes in national policy have produced or will produce new routine expectations about the place of religious groups in civic life; scholars are just now starting to ask these questions.[14]

Changes outside the realm of policy altogether may alter a regime of participation too. In the United States, immigration from non-Christian countries is one potential source of change. Observers such as religion scholar Rhys Williams suggest that the U.S. cultural mainstream itself may have to expand if it is going to incorporate newer groups into civic life. Religious communities outside of the Christian (and largely Protestant) tradition, he notes, face particular challenges in becoming civically active. They have to negotiate how, if at all, they should adopt the Protestant-style, congregation-like models of voluntary association that many American civic groups, secular as well as religious, take for granted as simply the way to run a good group. They have to achieve legitimacy with Judeo-Christian groups whose religious worldviews often share the liberal-individualist and universalist assumptions that dominate much of U.S. civic life. Is it becoming normal and unremarkable for non-Judeo-Christian groups to participate in local projects to advocate higher wages for striking workers, raise money for a new community center, shelter homeless people, or fight AIDS? We need more research to find out how groups less influenced by Protestant congregationalism or liberal individualism will accommodate the dominant civic group styles of the United States and how much the mainstream of U.S. civic culture itself will evolve through encounters with these different models, contributing to a new regime of participation.[15]

Research in this volume suggests that much of the relationship between the newer and the older participants in the American civic arena will have as much to do with the social *contexts* in which newer groups live and worship as with their particular religious beliefs. To guess these newer religious groups' civic prospects on the basis of their beliefs or doctrines alone is to risk, again, a kind of simple theological determinism. Certainly the specifics of religious traditions outside the Judeo-Christian tradition are relevant to the civic prospects of new Americans. Still, we should not estimate these Americans' likelihood of civic assimilation, accommodation, resistance, or separation solely by the relative distance of their religious beliefs from the dominant Christian ones.

Getting Beyond "Religion as First Mover": How Do Religious Commitment and Civic Participation Mutually Influence or Constitute Each Other?

We can learn a lot by studying how people juggle sacred and secular goods in civic groups—religious witness and political advocacy, for instance—instead of asking only how religion makes people do what they do. Researcher Ziad Munson found, for instance, that antiabortion protestors understood themselves as acting politically, not just religiously, when they prayed and demonstrated outside clinics. The protests weren't "really just politics" or "really just religious witness." They were both.[16]

Sometimes it is tempting for social scientists to err in the opposite direction and force normative, "civic" expectations onto religious groups that group members appreciate for their sacred goods, whether or not those goods also facilitate civic ends. It is not just an occupational hazard of Tocquevillians. Scholars in search of subordinate groups' resistance to social domination certainly can find it in public religious celebrations, and it is all the more obvious in the work of religious social justice activists and community organizers.[17] The danger is that in our zeal to identify critical consciousness and active resistance, we may risk underestimating the degree to which the people we write about understand themselves as enacting deeply religious action in the world that may also be political, not just politics with a religious motif.

In civic life people enjoy secular and sacred goods at the same time, sometimes in tension. Sometimes religious commitment changes in the civic fray. Although contemporary writers like to quote Tocqueville's claim that American religion would promote a civil, democratic public life, less often do we recall Tocqueville's companion claim that religion itself became more "civil" and democratic in the American civic and political context. In less sweeping terms, we may learn a lot by asking how people's own religious commitments change as a result of their experiences as activists or community leaders.[18]

Getting Beyond Beliefs: What Other Aspects of Culture Shape Civic Action in Religious Groups?

Religion is more than theologies and denominational traditions. Of course beliefs matter. Yet when religious beliefs create or influence civic life, they do so embedded in organizational formats, group styles, or customs—enduring ways of coordinating groups and defining what makes a good member. Sociologist Penny Edgell Becker found, for instance, that even churches of the same denomination in the same city sustained different relations to the wider community depending on the congregation's preferred organizational model.[19] Models or customs of group life filter, selectively focus, or silence aspects of religious traditions.[20] They bid members to favor some theological interpretations over others and some religious dictates over others.

Some of these group customs or organizational models sound wholly secular; others are closely identified with religious traditions such that we might consider them religious customs. Either way, they are not "religion" narrowly conceived as teachings derived directly from sacred texts. They may be integral to religious culture but are not theology. If we neglect these aspects of culture and religious culture beyond theological beliefs, we risk missing crucial factors in religion's civic power or irrelevance.[21]

How Do Religious Practices Vary in Different Settings or Relationships?

Religious people sometimes say and do quite different things in different civic settings with what looks "on paper" like the same religion. In some public settings, churchgoers may hardly sound religious at all.[22] Focusing on settings and relationships can help us avoid having to designate entire groups simply as "religious" or "not religious." The closer focus helps us describe more accurately what kinds of civic ties religious people create or what kinds of issues they can deliberate, where and when.[23] We can also more readily see how people *become* more or less religious-sounding in interactions throughout the life of an association.

By attending to settings and relationships rather than just groups, and by studying religious culture beyond beliefs alone, we can avoid the perils of a religious essentialism that colors much of the recent policy debate on "faith-based" groups. Opponents as well as advocates of religion in public life often have assumed that religious groups run on religious beliefs, that secular groups do not, and that either religious belief or its absence improves the chances for compassion and open-mindedness or judgment and divisiveness, depending on what the observer thinks about religion's potentials. A broader focus on religious culture and a closer focus on relationships forces us to encounter the more multifaceted reality that students of the civic life of religion are discovering when they get past religious essentialism.[24]

The civic life of American religion can be expansive, narrow, welcoming, exclusive, deeply character-changing, superficial, or fleeting. The questions outlined here can help to open up the civic life of religion to a wide variety of scholars, writers, and policymakers, including ones who do not identify as religion specialists. If religious people and traditions are a normal part of civic life, then scholars and citizens—all of us—benefit from including them in our terms of inquiry.

Notes

1. For information about religious organizations and voluntary associational memberships, see Wuthnow (2004).

2. For foundational statements on the public sphere, see Habermas (1989). For critical elaborations of the concept, see Calhoun (1992).

3. For more discussion of the difference between this "received Tocqueville" and the more ambivalent Tocqueville of *Democracy in America*, see Lichterman (2005, 2006).

4. Organizational sociologists in the "new institutionalism" have written at length about the role of widely shared, enduring narratives in legitimating and constructing organizations. See Powell and DiMaggio (1991). Briefly, the neo-institutionalist approach holds that organizations gain legitimacy and (all other things being equal) succeed when they can appear to conform to institutionalized understandings of what a bureaucracy, for instance (or in our case, a congregation) should be. But, as other neo-institutional writers have pointed out, there may be multiple or even competing institutionalized narratives in an organizational field. On this point, see Friedland and Alford (1991). Religious leaders who attempt to launch civic or politically oriented projects in a congregation do so in an environment where religious narratives about the congregation or the temple are powerful organizing principles for the collectivity, though they may not be the only rubrics that such groups draw from. Protestant Christian "mega-churches," for instance, may draw from corporate and bureaucratic narratives as well as from durable and widely shared understandings of what a congregation should be.

5. See, for example, Jason Kaufman's (2002) study of fraternal organizations in the "golden age" of American civic life. Kaufman found that lodges and fraternal orders competed fiercely for recruits. They adopted uniforms and badges and provided actuarial insurance for members, all in order to distinguish themselves from other orders and highlight particular ethnic, racial, or religious identities different from those associated with other orders.

6. For an overview of the "boundaries" approach, see Lamont and Molnár (2002).

7. On moral boundaries, see Lamont (1992). On distinctions between public and private, see Weintraub and Kumar (1997). On the vocabularies that shape religiously based political action, see Wood (2002).

8. On the cultural "group styles" that shape interaction in groups, see Eliasoph and Lichterman (2003). For recent advances in cultural sociology related to the topic of what can and cannot be said, see Alexander (2003) and Jacobs and Spillman (1995).

9. See Eliasoph (1998) and Walsh (2004).

10. On the history of critical debate in the Catholic Church that has the qualities of the best kind of public sphere, see Dillon (1999).

11. See Bellah et al. ([1985] 1996) and Wuthnow (1991).

12. See Orsi (1997) on this point.

13. See Berger and Luckmann (1967); on the organizational formats of religious life, see, for instance, Demerath et al. (1998); on congregations that borrow the folk understandings or group formats of group therapy, see Becker (1999) or Robert Bellah et al. ([1985] 1996).

14. See Chaves (1999) and Bane et al. (2000).

15. On this point see Williams (2007).

16. See Munson (2002).

17. See, for instance, Lancaster (1988).

18. See Hart (2001).

19. See Becker (1999).

20. See the extensive argument in Eliasoph and Lichterman (2003).

21. See Lichterman (2008, 2005), Becker (1999), and Cnaan et al. (2002).

22. See Bender (2003).

23. See Bender (2003) and Lichterman (2008). For a helpful argument about situated religious meanings that informs both of these works as well as our argument here, see Ammerman (2003).

24. See Wuthnow (2004).

Works Cited

Alexander, Jeffrey. 2003. *The Meanings of Social Life*. New York: Oxford University Press.

Ammerman, Nancy. 2003. "Religious Identities and Religious Institutions." In *Handbook for the Sociology of Religion*, M. Dillon, ed., 207–24. Cambridge: Cambridge University Press.

Bane, Mary Jo, Brent Coffin, and Ronald F. Thiemann. 2000. *Who Will Provide? The Changing Role of Religion in American Social Welfare*. Boulder, CO: Westview Press.

Becker, Penny. 1999. *Congregations in Conflict*. Cambridge: Cambridge University Press.

Bellah, Robert, Richard Madsen, William Sullivan, Ann Swidler, and Steven Tipton. [1985] 1996. *Habits of the Heart*. Updated edition with a new introduction. Berkeley: University of California Press.

Bender, Courtney. 2003. *Heaven's Kitchen: Living Religion at God's Love We Deliver.* Chicago: University of Chicago Press.

Berger, Peter, and Thomas Luckmann. 1967. *The Sacred Canopy.* New York: Anchor Books.

Calhoun, Craig, ed. 1992. *Habermas and the Public Sphere.* Chicago: University of Chicago Press.

Chaves, Mark. 1999. "Religious Congregations and Welfare Reform: Who Will Take Advantage of 'Charitable Choice'?" *American Sociological Review* 64:836–46.

Cnaan, Ram, with Stephanie C. Boddie, Femida Handy, Caynor Yancey, and Richard Schneider. 2002. *The Invisible Caring Hand: American Congregations and the Provision of Welfare.* New York: New York University Press.

Demerath, Nicholas J., Peter Dobkin Hall, Terry Schmitt, and Rhys H. Williams, eds. 1998. *Sacred Companies: Organizational Aspects of Religion and Religious Aspects of Organizations.* New York: Oxford University Press.

Dillon, Michele. 1999. "The Authority of the Holy Revisited: Habermas, Religion, and Emancipatory Possibilities." *Sociological Theory* 17: 290–306.

Eliasoph, Nina. 1998. *Avoiding Politics: How Americans Produce Apathy in Everyday Life.* New York: Cambridge University Press.

Eliasoph, Nina, and Paul Lichterman. 2003. "Culture in Interaction." *American Journal of Sociology* 108:735–94.

Friedland, Roger, and Robert R. Alford. 1991. "Bringing Society Back In: Symbols, Practices, and Institutional Contradictions." In *The New Institutionalism in Organizational Analysis,* Walter Powell and Paul DiMaggio, eds., 232–63. Chicago: University of Chicago Press.

Habermas, Jürgen. 1989. *The Structural Transformation of the Public Sphere.* Cambridge: MIT Press.

Hart, Stephen. 2001. *Cultural Dilemmas of Progressive Politics.* Chicago: University of Chicago Press.

Jacobs, Mark, and Lyn Spillman. 1995. "Cultural Sociology at the Crossroads of the Discipline." *Poetics* 33:1–14.

Kaufman, Jason. 2002. *For the Common Good?* New York: Oxford University Press.

Lamont, Michèle. 1992. *Money, Morals, and Manners.* Chicago: University of Chicago Press.

Lamont, Michèle, and Virág Molnár. 2002. "The Study of Boundaries in the Social Sciences." *Annual Review of Sociology* 28:167–95.

Lancaster, Roger. 1988. *Thanks to God and the Revolution.* New York: Columbia University Press.

Lichterman, Paul. 2005. *Elusive Togetherness: Church Groups Trying to Bridge America's Divisions.* Princeton, NJ: Princeton University Press.

————. 2006. "Social Capital or Group Style? Rescuing Tocqueville's Insights on Civic Engagement." *Theory and Society* 35:529–63.

————. 2008. "Religion and the Construction of Civic Identity." *American Sociological Review* 73:83–104.

Munson, Ziad. 2002. "Becoming an Activist: Believers, Sympathizers, and Mobilization in the American Pro-Life Movement." PhD diss., Harvard University.

Orsi, Robert. 1997. "Everyday Miracles: The Study of Lived Religion." In *Lived Religion in America: Towards a History of Practice*, D. Hall, ed., 3–21. Princeton, NJ: Princeton University Press.

Powell, Walter, and Paul DiMaggio, eds. 1991. *The New Institutionalism in Organizational Analysis*. Chicago: University of Chicago Press.

Toqueville, Alexis de. [1835] 1969. *Democracy in America*, edited by J. P. Mayer. Translated by G. Lawrence. Garden City, NY: Doubleday.

Walsh, Katherine Cramer. 2004. *Talking about Politics: Informal Groups and Social Identity in American Life*. Chicago: University of Chicago Press.

Weintraub, Jeffrey, and Krishnan Kumar, eds. 1997. *Public and Private in Thought and Practice: Perspectives on a Grand Dichotomy*. Chicago: University of Chicago Press.

Williams, Rhys. 2007. "The Languages of the Public Sphere: Religious Pluralism, Institutional Logics, and Civil Society." *The Annals of the American Academy of Political and Social Science* 612:42–61.

Wood, Richard. 2002. *Faith in Action*. Chicago: University of Chicago Press.

Wuthnow, Robert. 1991. *Acts of Compassion*. Princeton, NJ: Princeton University Press.

————. 2004. *Saving America? Faith-Based Services and the Future of Civil Society*. Princeton, NJ: Princeton University Press.

Index

Abortion rights, 38–39
Academic study: civic participation and, 147–52; community studies and, 8–9; religious associations and, 5, 11–15
Activist practices, 54
Adopt-a-Family program, 104–5, 105–6, 107–11, 115
Affinity groups, 88
African American churches, 59, 83, 88
African Americans, religious discourse and, 113
Alcoholics Anonymous, 31
Alexander, Jeffrey, 16n13
American Civil Liberties Union, 30
American Nuclear Society, 34
American Time Use Survey, 79
Ammerman, Nancy, 5, 12, 14, 96n6, 142, 143–44
Anderson, Elijah, 97n8
Anti-abortion movement, 150
Anti-political rhetoric, congregations and, 124. See also Political discourse
Anti-pornography activists, 104
Anti-poverty efforts, 9
Arts, the, 12, 74–77, 78–79, 141
Association for Retarded Citizens, 31
Atheists, 10, 50
Attendance, at church services, 50, 63n8. See also Religious participation
Azusa Christian Community, 91–93, 94

Baby boomers, individualism and, 37–38
Baker House. See Ella J. Baker House

Ballots, 25
Bane, Mary Jo, 101
Baptist Church, 130
Becker, Penny Edgell, 150–51
Bellah, Robert, 7, 101, 105
Berger, Peter, 1, 147
Biblical language: religious discourse and, 112, 113, 145; secular society and, 8
Biblical teachings, homosexuality and, 127, 128, 137n11
Bimber, Bruce, 35
Bisexuality, 137n8
Bloom, Allan, 40
B'nai B'rith, 3
"Body of Christ," 8
Bonding capital, 52–53, 94. See also Social capital
Book of Discipline (United Methodist Church), 124–25, 137n5
Boundaries: religious associations and, 13, 15, 141; religious districts, 91–94; urban churches and, 86
Bridge building civic functions, 59–60, 94; congregations and, 144, 149
Budgets, congregational, 71
Bush, George W., 6, 111, 118n8

Carroll, Jackson, 74–75
Carter, Stephen, 105
Casanova, José, 17n20, 49
Chambers of commerce, 36
"Charitable Choice" program, 6, 105, 108
Charitable works. See Volunteer work

Charity, justice and, 114
Chaves, Mark, 6, 12–13, 103, 143–44
Choice, religious: civic participation and, 147, 148; political discourse and, 131; religious discourse, in the public square and, 103; urban churches and, 88–89
Christian conservatives, 2, 5. *See also* Conservative churches
Christian fundamentalists, 117
Christian Identity movements, 52
Christianity: communal cohesion and, 8; political discourse and, 127–28; religious discourse, in the public square and, 108, 109–10
"Church as savior" modes, 85–86
Churches. *See* Congregations; Religious associations
"Church people," religious discourse and, 114
Church shopping, 88–89, 147
Citizenship, 1, 24–27
Civic connections: long-term connections, 71, 142; "loose" connections, 7; religious districts and, 91–94
Civic groups: civic participation and, 141–42; civil rights movement and, 40; communication and, 6; membership of, 2–3; professional management of, 6–7; religious associations as, 4; temporary civic groups, 29
Civic lens, religious associations and, 4–10
Civic life, definition of, 2–4
Civic participation: congregations and, 53–58, 69–70; denominations and, 60–61; historical perspective on, 11–12; ideal forms of, 27–31; individualism and, 37–40; length of, 35–37; non-Christian religious traditions and, 149; political discourse and, 123, 125–26, 135–36; religious associations and, 4–10, 151–52; religious beliefs and, 150; religious discourse, in the public square and, 116; religious districts and, 82–96, 87–88; risk and sacrifice and, 40–44; therapeutic groups and NIMBYs, 31–35; varieties of, 23–27, 44–45. *See also* Participation rates
Civic skills. *See* Skills, for civic participation
Civility, 45, 48, 62n5, 135–36
"Civil religion," 50, 61
Civil rights movement, 2, 26, 39, 40

Civil society, 3–4
Civil Society, Civic Engagement and Catholicism in the U.S. (Liedhegener and Kremp), 80
Class action lawsuits, 39
Clergy, child sexual abuse and, 40
Clothing programs, 71
Coffin, Brent, 101
Collaboration, between government and religious organizations, 116. *See also* "Faith-based initiatives"
Collective action, churches and, 90
Colonial era, civic participation and, 24–25
Commercial activities, religious districts and, 83, 89
Common good, the, 7, 8, 17n20, 48–62
Communal cohesion, religious associations and, 8
Communal sentiment, unorganized, 45–46n5
Communication: civic groups and, 6; civic participation and, 141, 151–52; digital communication and, 35; political discourse and, 123–36; religious associations and, 11; religious beliefs and, 147. *See also* Religious discourse, in the public square
Communicative rationality, 134–36, 137–38n16
Community boundaries. *See* Boundaries
Community building: congregations and, 12, 13, 52–53, 59–60; event-centered civic activities and, 36–37; religious associations and, 11; religious districts and, 82, 83; therapeutic groups and, 31–32
Community development programs, 89–90
Community involvement, predictors of, 57
Community life, urban churches and, 95
Community organizations, religious discourse, in the public square and, 104
Community studies, 8–9
Competition, religious districts and, 88
Conflict: civic participation and, 142; congregations and, 60; political discourse and, 124, 129, 131, 132, 132–33, 135
Congregational life, religious associations and, 53–58
Congregations: the arts and, 74–77, 78–79; civic life and, 4, 12, 53–58, 69–70; civic participation and, 12–13, 53–58, 143–44; intercongregational alliances, 13–14;

"new institutionalism" and, 152n4; organizational needs of, 14, 61–62; political activity and, 58–59; political discourse and, 128–34; religious choice and, 148; religious deliberation and, 14, 104–17; social service activities of, 70–75, 77, 79–80, 102–3; therapeutic groups and, 33; urbanism and, 87; voluntary associations and, 147

Conservative churches, 115, 125, 145

Conversations, personal. See Religious discourse, in the public square

Cooley, Charles, 84

Corporations, civic participation and, 34, 39

Courts, the. See Litigation

Criminal justice system, religious districts and, 92

Cultural literacy, religious imagery and, 8

Culture, religion in, 14–15, 146–47

Culture wars, 10, 18n32, 100, 125, 145

Dahl, Robert, 26

Dance, congregations and, 76

Day of the Dead celebrations, 36–37

Dean, Howard, 35

Delacroix, Al, 130–31

Deliberation, constraints on, 14, 56, 115, 142, 144–45

Demerath, Nicholas J., 61

Democracy in America (Tocqueville), 140

Democratic processes, 34, 101–2; civic groups and, 6–7; resource distribution and, 95, 96. See also Political activities

Demographic changes, 44

Demographics, urban churches and, 86

Denominational politics, United Methodist Church and, 125–26

Denominations, in the U.S., 51–52, 56, 60–61, 114–15. See also specific denominations

Development, of religious districts, 88–89

DiIulio, John, 118n8

Dillon, Michelle, 137–38n16

Diminished Democracy (Skocpol), 27

Disaster response, 57–58

Disestablishment of religion, 49, 51, 102–4, 148

Dispositions, personal, 42–43, 48–49

Dissenting positions, political discourse and, 125, 126, 135

Diversity, congregations and, 59–60, 60–62

Doctrine, religious, 14

Domestic violence, 42

Drake, St. Clair, 96n6

Drama. See Theatrical performances

Economic development, religious districts and, 91

Educational politics. See Informational politics

Elections, presidential, 111

Eliasoph, Nina, 43–44, 123

Elks clubs, 3

Ella J. Baker House, 92–93

Employment: civic participation and, 41–42; development of civic skills and, 78; in social service programs, 71, 75

Employment programs, 71

Empowerment, of citizens, 7

Environmentalism, 34

Environmental Protection Agency, 34

Essentialism, of religious beliefs, 146–47, 151

Ethnic groups, 36–37

Etzioni, Amitai, 7

Europe, religious associations and, 38, 148–49

Evangelical churches, 52, 54, 58–59, 107–11. See also Christian fundamentalists; conservative churches

Event-centered civic activities, 29, 30, 35–37, 40, 57–58, 142

Evil, political discourse and, 128–29

Exclusivity. See Inclusivity vs. exclusivity

Ex-gay movements, 137n14

Exodus story, 8

Faith, urban churches and, 92–93

"Faith-based initiatives": essentialism, of religious beliefs and, 151; public policy and, 6, 79–80; religious discourse, in the public square and, 116–17; religious districts and, 95–96; social bonds and, 118n8; social services and, 9, 69, 70, 73; welfare reform and, 105

Fellowship activities, 53, 54, 60, 93, 94, 144

Feminism, political discourse and, 129–30

Financial contributions, 40

Fish, John, 96n6

Fish, Stanley, 48

Food programs, 71, 72, 73, 77

Ford, Betty, 43

Foundational assumptions: civic participation and, 145; political discourse and, 123, 124, 133–34, 134–35
Four Corners neighborhood, Boston, 82–83, 90–91, 91–92, 93
Fragmentation, of civic life, 13. *See also* Social bonds
Frankness, in public discourse, 43–44
Fraser, Nancy, 112
Fraternal organizations, 2–3, 144, 152n5
Fukuyama, Francis, 7
Functional diffusion, congregations and, 60
Fundementalists. *See* Christian fundamentalists

Gamm, Gerald, 96n6
Gangs, religious districts and, 92
Gay and lesbian inclusion, 14. *See also* Homosexuality
God, Sex and Politics: Homosexuality and Everyday Theologies (Moon), 124
God-talk. *See* Religious discourse, in the public square
Golden Rule practices, 54
Good Citizen, The (Schudson), 24
Governmental action, 3, 38, 51, 148–49. *See also* Disestablishment of religion
Government services: congregations and, 72–73, 77; neighborhoods and, 90; religious discourse, in the public square and, 107, 108, 110, 111. *See also* "Faith-based initiatives"
Grand Army of the Republic, 25, 27
Grange, the, 27
Grants, event-centered civic activities and, 36
Greenpeace, 3
Grey Panthers, 3
Group identity, 110–11, 113–14, 145, 150–51
Group styles, 153n8
Growing Divide workshops, 112, 113
Gun-control legislation, 35

Habermas, Jürgen, 101, 137–38n16
Habitat for Humanity, 71, 73
Hannerz, Ulf, 96n7
Health programs, 71
Hegel, G. W. F., 16n13
Historical perspective: on civic life, 11–12; civic participation and, 24–27, 142; religious districts and, 88–89

Holmes, Stephen, 38
Homeless persons, programs for, 71
Homosexuality: civic participation and, 142, 145; coming out and, 42; religious associations and, 24, 40; United Methodist Church and, 123–36
Housing and shelter programs, 71, 73
Hunter, James, 18n32

Idealism, political discourse and, 132–33
Identity politics, 7
Immigrant rights movement, 56
Immigrants: civic participation and, 149; religious districts and, 83
"In All Things Charity" petition, 126–27, 128
Inclusivity vs. exclusivity: congregations and, 52–53, 59–60; political discourse and, 133; religious associations and, 52–53
Individualism: civic participation and, 26, 30, 37–40, 42–43, 44, 142; non-Christian religious traditions and, 149; religious associations and, 15, 31; therapeutic groups and, 32–33; Tocquevillian celebration and, 140
Individual rights. *See* Rights, individual
Individuals, society and, 84–85
Informational politics, 25–26
"Informed citizen, the," 25, 26–27
Injustice, speaking up against, 43
Institutional contexts, 12, 13
Interest groups, civic participation and, 25–26
Internal imperatives. *See* Organizational needs
Internet, the, 35
Interorganizational connections, 13–14, 57, 62

Janowitz, Morris, 90
Jesus, social action and, 113
Judaism, 8
Justice, charity and, 114
Justice Task Force, 104, 105, 112–15

Kaufman, Jason, 2–3, 152n5
King, Martin Luther, Jr., 40
Kremp, Werner, 80

Lakeburg, local voluntary associations in, 104–15
Language, religious. *See* Religious discourse, in the public square

Latino Americans, 36–37
Lawyers, civic participation and, 30, 39
Leadership skills, 56. *See also* Skills, for civic
    participation
League of Women Voters, 3, 25
Length, of civic participation, 35–37, 35–37,
    44
Liberal churches: civic participation and,
    54, 145; political discourse and, 125;
    religious discourse, in the public square
    and, 112–15; volunteer work and, 63n8.
    See also Protestant churches
Lichterman, Paul, 13–14, 14–15, 58, 136–37n3,
    141, 144–45
Liedhegener, Antonius, 80
Litigation, 30, 32, 38–39, 39–40
Local chapters of national organizations, 28
Local voluntary associations. *See* Voluntary
    associations
Long-term civic connections, 71, 142
"Loose" civic connections, 7
Los Angeles riots (1992), 57–58, 142
Luckmann, Thomas, 1, 147

Mainline Protestant churches. *See* Liberal
    churches; Protestant churches
Manners, democratic spirit of, 42–43
Marches on Washington, 29
Marchi, Regina, 36
Market forces, civic groups and, 3
Marx, Karl, 16n13, 96n7
McGerr, Michael, 25–26
McRoberts, Omar, 13, 15, 141, 144, 146
Media, 4, 25, 117, 145
Membership: in civic groups, 2–3, 15–16n3,
    16–17n16; congregations and, 53, 148;
    event-centered civic activities and, 35;
    fraternal organizations and, 152n5
Million Mom March, 35
Mobility, churches and, 90–91
Monotheism, 62n5
Moon, Dawne, 5–6, 14–15, 141, 145
Moral concerns, social movements and, 28
Moral order: civic participation and, 141–42;
    religious districts and, 87, 94–95; urban
    churches and, 84, 85–86, 92, 93–94
Moral posturing, civic participation
    and, 40
Moral reform ministries, 86, 96n4
Mosques. *See* Congregations
Mothers Against Drunk Driving, 3, 31

Motivations, for civic participation, 150
Munson, Ziad, 55
Music, congregations and, 74, 76, 78–79
Mutual aid societies, 2–3
Myths, about congregational activities, 70–73

NAACP (National Association for the Ad-
    vancement of Colored People), 39
"Naked" public square, 101, 105
National Congregations Study, 12, 70, 75
National governments, religious associa-
    tions and, 148
National voluntary organizations. *See* Vol-
    untary associations
Natural ecology, urban processes and,
    84–85
Negative contributions, to civic life. *See*
    Pessimistic perspective on religion in
    civic life
Neighborhoods: congregations and, 13;
    networks and, 89–91; religious districts
    and, 82–96, 144; residential demograph-
    ics and, 86; urban processes and, 85, 95
Networks. *See* Social networks
Neuhaus, Richard John, 101, 105, 111
"New institutionalism," 152n4
Newspapers, 25
NIMBY (Not In My Backyard) groups, 29,
    33–35
1960s, the, 1
Non-Christian religious traditions, 149
Non-profit organizations, 41, 72, 77
Norms, civic engagement and, 9–10

Odd Fellows, the, 27
Office of Faith-Based and Community
    Initiatives, 118n8
Optimistic perspective on religion in civic
    life, 9–10, 48–49, 61, 140–43
Ordination, United Methodist Church and,
    124, 126
Organizational models, civic participation
    and, 150–51
Organizational needs: civic participation
    and, 143–44; congregations and, 12, 14,
    59; intercongregational alliances and,
    13; religious associations and, 143; U.S.
    denominations and, 51–52, 52–53, 61–62
Organizational structure: national volun-
    tary organizations and, 28; political
    parties and, 29

Parachurches, event-centered civic activities and, 37
Park, Robert, 84
Parsons, Talcott, 1, 16n13
Participation rates: in arts activities, 74–75, 75–76, 78–79, 80n1; attendance at church services, 50, 63n8; in political activities, 76, 77–78, 80n1; in social service programs, 71, 76–77, 79, 80n1. *See also* Civic participation
Partisanship, civic participation and, 25
Partnerships. *See* Interorganizational connections
Pastoral narrative, 85
Paxton, Pamela, 56–57
Peace activists, 104
Pessimistic perspective on religion in civic life, 10, 140–43
Petitions, political discourse and, 126–28, 134
Pluralism, 51, 62
Political activities: civic participation and, 24, 37–38; colonial era and, 24–25; congregations and, 12, 58–59, 61, 73–74, 79; event-centered civic activities and, 35–36, 37; frankness and, 43–44; litigation and, 39–40; national voluntary organizations and, 28; NIMBY (Not In My Backyard) groups and, 34; participation rates in, 76, 77–78; religious associations and, 2, 5–6, 9, 140–41; religious beliefs and, 55, 150; religious discourse in the public square and, 1, 105–6, 109, 111; therapeutic groups and, 31, 32
Political discourse, 14, 50, 123–36, 145
Political organizations, 77–78
Political parties, 25–26, 28–29, 41, 45, 59
Positive contributions, to civic life. *See* Optimistic perspective on religion in civic life
Postbureaucratic organizations, 35
"Post-secular" society, 101
Poverty, 82, 87, 95–96, 109
Pragmatist philosophy, 84–85
Prayer, 110, 111
Private sphere: civic participation and, 42–43; frankness and, 43–44; religion and, 1, 8–9, 13–14; religious discourse in the public square and, 103
Professional management, of civic groups, 3, 6–7, 28, 29–30, 41

Progressive Era, 25–26
Promise Keepers, 37, 129–30
Property rights, 38
Proselytizing, 104–5, 108. *See also* Religious discourse, in the public square
Protestant churches, 17n25, 59, 112–15
Public arenas, congregations' contributions to, 75–80
Public interest groups, 49
Public life, religion in, 1
Public opinion, 50
Public policy: civic participation and, 28–29; "faith-based initiatives" and, 79–80; religious associations and, 13–14, 49; religious discourse in the public square and, 108, 109. *See also* Government services
Public purposes, insufficient orientation to, 31–35, 44
Public square: disestablishment of religion and, 102–4; religious contributions to, 100–102, 115–17; religious discourse and, 13–14, 104–15. *See also* Private sphere
Putnam, Robert: baby boomers and, 37–38; civic participation and, 7, 23–24, 27, 44, 142; religious discourse and, 101; social capital and, 9; therapeutic groups and, 30, 31–32

"Radius of trust," civic groups and, 7
Rationality, religion and, 48, 62n1, 100, 101
Religious associations: changing denominations and, 44; civic participation and, 4–10, 24, 140–41; civil rights movement and, 40; the common good and, 17n20, 48–62; congregational life and, 53–58; event-centered civic activities and, 37; inclusivity vs. exclusivity, 52–53; individualism and, 31; political activity and, 5–6, 58–59; secular society and, 146; social services and, 77; therapeutic groups and, 32, 33; United States and, 49–52. *See also* Congregations
Religious beliefs: civic participation and, 141, 143, 150; essentialism of, 146–47; political activity and, 55; religious discourse, in the public square and, 106; social issues and, 102–4, 126–28, 135; in the United States, 49–50

Religious discourse, in the public square: civic participation and, 151–52; disestablishment of religion and, 102–4; local examples of, 104–15; religious contributions to, 100–102, 115–17
Religious districts: boundaries and, 91–94; civic participation and, 141, 144; development of, 88–89; neighborhood civic life and, 82–84, 89–91, 94–96; urban processes and, 84–88, 94–96
Religious ecology, 85
Religious economy, 103, 115
Religious education, 52, 61, 73, 74, 75
Religious identity, 102, 106, 110, 114, 115, 116–17
Religious imagery, 8
Religious participation, 55–56, 61–62
Religious particularism, 89
Religious symbolism, 104
Renaldi, Linda, 135, 136
Reparations, 39
Republican Party, 59
Resource Conservation and Recovery Act (1976), 34
Resource distribution, politics and, 95, 96
Rights, individual, 38, 142
Risk and sacrifice, civic participation and, 28, 40–44
Rivers, Eugene, 92, 93
Roe v. Wade (1973), 38
Roman Catholic Church, 56, 59, 63n8, 114, 153n10
Rosenblum, Nancy, 42–43
Rotary Club, 15–16n3, 144

Safire, William, 33–34
Sager, Rebecca, 72
Same-sex unions: individual rights and, 39; United Methodist Church and, 124, 126, 132
Sampson, Robert, 90
Schudson, Michael, 4, 11–12, 14, 142
Secular activities, urban churches and, 92
Secularism, political discourse and, 127–28
Secularization thesis, 103
Secular society, 101, 113, 146, 150–51
Self-help groups. See Therapeutic groups
Self-segregation, civic groups and, 3
September 11 attacks, 32, 58
Sermons, political activity and, 58–59
Servanthood. See "Social servants"

Settings, for religious discourse, 115, 151–52
Sexuality, 124–25. See also Homosexuality
Shafer, Ruthie, 132–33
Shelter programs. See Housing and shelter programs
Short-term needs, programs for, 71. See also Event-centered civic activities
Simpsons, The, civic participation and, 24–27
Sites of the public sphere, 112
Skills, for civic participation, 56, 61–62, 78, 79, 102–3
Skocpol, Theda: civic participation and, 27, 44, 142; ideal forms of civic participation and, 23–24; professional management and, 6–7, 29–30, 41; religious discourse in the public square and, 101, 101–2
"Small-group movement," 33
Smith, Christian, 103
Social action: civic groups and, 3; political discourse and, 130–31; religious associations and, 4, 9, 11; urban churches and, 84
Social activities, 24, 25, 28
Social bonds, 101, 118n8, 140
Social capital, 7, 9–10, 16n15, 93, 94
Social change, 123–36, 149
Social classes: religious associations and, 10; religious districts and, 83, 88, 89; voluntary associations and, 28; volunteer work and, 58
Social critic identity, 114, 117
Social Gospel movement, 69–70, 75, 86, 96n4
Social isolation, therapeutic groups and, 31
Social issues, religious beliefs and, 102–4
Social movements, civic participation and, 26, 28
Social networks, 87, 89–91, 144
"Social servants," 110–11, 117
Social service programs, participation rates in, 76–77, 79
Social services: congregations and, 12, 13, 70–75, 77, 79–80; professional management and, 41; religious associations and, 5, 6, 15, 17n25, 49; religious discourse in the public square and, 104–15; religious districts and, 92–93, 95; religious participation and, 140–41; urban churches and, 86

Sociology: religion in public life and, 1, 2; religious beliefs and, 146–47; urban churches and, 84–85, 94; urbanization and, 84–88
Speaking up, civic participation and, 43
Spirituality, 53, 94
State, the. *See* Governmental action
Storefront churches, 13, 82, 83
"Street, the," 91–92, 91–94, 97n8, 144
Streets of Glory (McRoberts), 82, 83–84
Subaltern public, 112
Subcultures, urbanism and, 87
Substance abuse programs, 71
Suffering, religious districts and, 87
Sunstein, Cass, 38
Suttles, Gerald, 90
Symbolic boundaries, 91–94, 144
Synagogues. *See* Congregations

Task force meetings, 112
Task-oriented volunteer activities, 109, 111
Taxes, religious associations and, 6
Television personalities, religious discourse and, 117, 145
Temporary civic groups, 29
Theatrical performances, 74, 76
"The More Excellent Way: God's Plan Re-Affirmed" petition, 126–28
Theology. *See* Religious beliefs
Therapeutic groups, 30, 31–33, 153n13
Thiemann, Ronald, 101
Thomas, William, 84
Time commitments, 28, 74–75, 79
Tocqueville, Alexis de, 5, 6, 8, 14, 100, 140
Tocquevillian celebration, 11–15, 140, 141–42, 144
Transgendered persons, 137n8
Truths, enduring, 127–28, 128–29

United Methodist Church, 14, 123–36
United States context, religious associations and, 49–52, 148–49
Unity, political discourse and, 132–33

"Urbanism as a Way of Life" (Wirth), 86–87
Urban processes, religious districts and, 84–88, 94–96

Values, cultural, 1, 2, 8, 63n7
Values, religious, 124
Ventura, Jesse, 35
Venues, for activities, 77
Verba, Sidney, 77–78
Violence, against religious communities, 51
Voluntarism. *See* Choice, urban churches and
Voluntary associations: civic participation and, 3, 27–28, 142, 143; congregations and, 147; internal imperatives of, 144; non-Christian religious traditions and, 149; religious discourse in the public square and, 101, 102, 104–15
Volunteer work: attendance at church services and, 63n8; baby boomers and, 38; congregations and, 61–62, 72, 73, 79; Golden Rule practices and, 54; religious associations and, 4, 5, 11, 102; religious identity and, 116; religious participation and, 55–56, 57, 140–41; social classes and, 58; within U.S. denominations, 51, 52; voluntary associations and, 28, 42
Voter participation, 24–25, 28, 37
Voting guides, evangelical churches and, 59

Warner, Stephen, 51, 60, 61
Warren, Mark E., 16n13
Washington, George, 48–49
Weber, Max, 10, 62n1, 96n2
Welfare reform, 6, 9, 104, 107–11, 148–49
White flight, 85, 89
Wirth, Louis, 86–87
Wolfe, Alan, 37
Women's rights, 38–39, 40
Worship, 53, 61, 73
Wuthnow, Robert, 7, 33, 58, 77

Youth services, 92–93